DEATH SENTENCE

Don Watson

Death Sentence
THE DECAY OF PUBLIC LANGUAGE

KNOPF

Extract from *A Farewell to Arms* by Ernest Hemingway published by Jonathan Cape, used by permission of The Random House Group. Extract from *Other People's Trades* by Primo Levi reprinted by permission of Simon & Schuster Adult Publishing Group. Extract from *The Needs of Strangers* by Michael Ignatieff published by Chatto & Windus, used by permission of The Random House Group. Extract from *On Revolution* by Hannah Arendt published by Viking, used by permission of Penguin Putnam Inc. Extract from *Essays in English History* by AJP Taylor published by Penguin, used by permission of David Higham Associates.

A Knopf book
Published by Random House Australia Pty Ltd
20 Alfred Street, Milsons Point, NSW 2061
http://www.randomhouse.com.au

Sydney   New York   Toronto
London   Auckland   Johannesburg

First published in 2003

National Library of Australia
Cataloguing-in-Publication Entry

Watson, Don, 1949– .
Death sentence : the decay of public language.

ISBN 1 74051 206 5.

1. English language – Australia – Usage. 2. English language – Social aspects – Australia. 3. Sociolinguistics – Australia. 4. Language and culture – Australia. I. Title.

Cover illustration by William T. Cooper
Cover design by Yolande Gray
Internal design by Yolande Gray
Printed and bound by Griffin Press, Netley, South Australia

10 9

Don't you see that the whole aim of Newspeak is to
narrow the range of thought?
George Orwell,
1984

Language most shows a man: speak that I may see thee.
Ben Jonson

A great ox stands on my tongue.
Aeschylus,
Agamemnon

Introduction

Over the coming twelve months we will be
enhancing our product offering to bring you
new features and access to innovative funds.
You can be confident that our commitment
is resolute, to make changes that investor's
(sic) value.

Insurance company newsletter

PUBLIC LANGUAGE CONFRONTS MOST of us every day of our
lives, but rarely when we are with friends or family. Not
yet, at least. It is not the language in which we address
lovers, postmen, children or pets. So far.

True, in the households of young professionals they
will say sometimes that the new dog *adds alpha to their
lifestyle*; that they need *closure* with their orthodontist or
mother; that they are *empowered* by their Nikes. There
is seepage from the public to the private. But that's all it
is. *At this point in time*.

Public language is the language of public life: the
language of political and business leaders and civil
servants – official, formal, sometimes elevated language.
It is the language of leaders more than the led, the managers rather than the managed. It takes very different
forms: from shapely rhetoric to shapeless, enervating
sludge; but in every case it is the language of power and
influence. What our duties are, for whom we should vote,

which mobile phone plan we should take up: in all these places the public language rules. As power and influence are pervasive so is the language: we hear and read it at the highest levels and the lowest. And while it begins with the powerful, the weak are often obliged to speak it, imitate it. 'Even politicians speak/truths of value to the weak', Auden said. Believing as they do that everyone needs something even if they don't know it, marketing people would agree.

The influence of marketing shows itself in advertising and commerce, where we would expect to find it, and in politics and war, where its presence might surprise us. Marketing goes wherever the media goes and the media goes pretty well everywhere. Naturally the language goes too, which is why all kinds of institutions cannot pass on the simplest information about their services without also telling us that they are *contemporary, innovative and forward-looking* and *committed to continuous improvement*, as if the decision to raise their rates or change their phone number can only be grasped in this *context-sensitive* way. To help us all get going in the same direction they might give the context a name, like *Growing Victoria Together* or *Business Line Plus*, or *Operation Decapitation* where the service is a military one.

Managerialism, a name for various doctrines of business organisation, also comes with a language of its own, and to such unlikely places as politics and education. Even if the organisational principles of management or marketing were so widely appropriate, it is by no means certain that their language is. Marketing, for instance, has no particular concern with truth. Management concerns are relatively narrow – relative, that is, to life, knowledge and possibility. This alone makes marketing and managerial language less than ideal for a democracy or a college. In addition their language lacks almost everything needed to put in words an opinion or an emotion; to explain the complex, paradoxical or uncertain; to tell a joke. If those who propagate this muck really believed in being *context-sensitive*, they would understand that in the context of ordinary human need and sensibility their language is extraordinarily *in*sensitive. It enrages, depresses, humiliates, confuses. It leaves us speechless.

Public language that defies normal understanding is, as Primo Levi wrote, 'an ancient repressive artifice, known to all churches, the typical vice of our political class, the foundation of all colonial empires'. They will tell you it is in the interests of leadership, management, efficiency, *stakeholders*, the *bottom line* or some democratic imperative, but the public language remains the language of power. It has its origins in the subjection or control of one by another. In all societies, 'To take power is to win speech'. Whatever its appearance, intimidation and manipulation come as naturally to public language as polite instruction, information and enlightenment. That is why vigilance is needed: an argument concerning the public language is an argument concerning liberty.

To Levi's list of obfuscating types we could add many sociologists and deconstructionists, including some who design school curricula and courses with the word 'Studies' in them. The politically correct might have a case to answer for years of philistine abuse (often, strangely, in the name of cultures), had the Prime Minister not abolished them. We are now all free, he says, to speak our minds; but the language continues to decay, which rather lets political correctness off the hook. Political correctness and its equally irritating twin, anti-political correctness; economic rationalism; dope-smoking; Knowledge Management – wherever cults exist the language inclines to the arcane or inscrutable. This is no bad thing of itself, but obnoxious in a democratic or educational environment. Among Druids, Masons or economists we expect the language to be unfathomable or at least unclear or strange. They speak in code. This can only be because they do not want us to understand, or do not themselves understand, or are so in the habit of speaking this way they have lost the ability to communicate normally. When we hear this sort of language it is, therefore, common sense to assume there is a cult, or something like a cult, in the vicinity. And be alert, if not alarmed.

While English spreads across the globe, the language itself is shrinking. Vast numbers of new words enter it every year, but our children's and leaders' vocabularies are getting smaller. Latin and Greek have been squeezed out of most journalists' English and 'obscure' words are forbidden unless they qualify as economic or business jargon. You write for your audience and your audience knows fewer words than it used to and hasn't time to look up unfamiliar ones. The language of politics is tuned to the same audience and uses the same media to reach it, so it too diminishes year by year. *Downsized*, business would say. Business language is a desert. Like a public company, the public language is being trimmed of excess and subtlety; what it doesn't need is shed, what is useful is reorganised, *prioritised* and attached either to new words or to old ones stripped of meaning. In business, language is now *productivity-driven*.

What of the media whose words we read and hear every day? The code of conduct of the International Federation of Journalists is categorical: 'Respect for the truth and the right of the public to truth is the first duty of the journalist.' There can be no respect for the truth without respect for the language. Only when language is alive does truth have a chance. As the powerful in legend turn the weak or the vanquished into stone, they turn us to stone through language. This is the essential function of a cliché, and of cant and jargon; to neutralise expression and 'vanish memory'. They are dead words. They will not do for truth.

Therefore, to live according to their code, journalists must choose their own words carefully and skilfully and insist that others do the same. The proper relationship of journalists to the public language is that of unrelenting critics. It is their duty to see through it. But we cannot rely on them. Norman Mailer once wrote on behalf of writers like himself that 'the average reporter could not get a sentence straight if it were phrased more subtly than his own mind could make phrases'. They munched nuances 'like peanuts', he said. True, it happens and it's maddening, but inadequate prose is still journalism and roughly meets the requirements of the code. It is something else, however, when journalists ignore abuses of the public language by people of influence and power, and reproduce without comment words that are intended to deceive and manipulate. When this happens journalism ceases to be journalism and becomes a kind of propaganda; or a reflection of what Simone Weil called 'the superb indifference that the powerful have for the weak'.

The war in Iraq provided a case in point. The military provided brand names – *Shock and Awe*, for instance – and much of the media could see nothing but to use them. Each day of the campaign the media were briefed in the language of the Pentagon's media relations people, whereupon very often the journalists briefed their audiences in the same language. The media centre in Doha was always *on message*, and so was the media. When the military said they had *degraded* by 70 per cent a body of Iraqi soldiers, this was what the media reported. Few said 'killed' and only the Iraqi Minister for Information in his daily self-satire said 'slaughtered', which was a more honest word but a blatant lie because he said it of American soldiers, not Iraqi ones. One journalist, who knew something about the effects of Daisy Cutter bombs, said 'pureed'. And no one showed any pictures of the bodies. To be *embedded* with the Coalition forces was to be *embedded* in their language and their *message*. It turned out that *embedded* just meant 'in bed with' in the old language. If they said they had *attrited* an enemy force, generally that was what the media conveyed, and it was the same if they said *deconflicted*. All this was a sad retreat from both the journalists' code of conduct and the noble achievements of twentieth-century war reporting. Just as significant was the way these words spoke for the willingness of journalists to join the military in denying the common humanity of ordinary soldiers – especially the largely conscripted cannon fodder – on the opposing side. Here was another retreat: from war reporting standards going back to Homer.

The public language will only lift in tone and clarity when those who write and speak it take words seriously again. They need to tune their ears to it. Awareness is the only defence against the creeping plague of which this is a microscopic specimen. *The inquiry may allow for relevant businesses or industries to be identified and for investigation into the possibility that certain regional or rural areas of the state would be more affected than others.* No doubt in the place from which these words came they were judged competent. But they are not competent in the world at large. They are not competent as language. They represent an example of what George Orwell described as anaesthetic writing. You cannot read it without losing some degree of consciousness. You come to, and read it again, and still your brain will not reveal the meaning – will not even try. You are getting sleepy again. Read aloud, in a speech for instance, an audience hears the words as they might hear a plane passing overhead or a television in another room. We can easily make it sound less like a distant aeroplane by the simple expedient of saying it as if we mean it: *The inquiry will decide which businesses are relevant and which parts of the state will be badly affected.* In fact, to guess at the intended meaning, it might come down to *the Inquiry deciding which businesses and which parts of the state will be most affected.*

Of course, it's just one sentence. But we have to begin somewhere.

We must keep it in perspective of course. The decay or near death of language is not life threatening. It can be an aid to crime and tragedy; it can give us the reasons for unreasoning behaviour, including war and genocide and even famine. Words are deadly. Words are bullets. But a word is not a Weapon of Mass Destruction, or a jihad, or unhappiness. Like a rock, it is not a weapon (or a grinding stone) until someone picks it up and uses it as one. We should not get cranky or obsessive about words. You can't eat them, or buy things with them, or protect your borders with them, and it will not do to make a great display of your concern. There are more important things to think about than what we say or how we say it.

In any case resistance is probably futile: as futile as the Luddites' resistance was futile. Managerial language may well be to the information age what the machine and the assembly line were to the industrial. It is mechanised language. Like a machine, it removes the need for thinking: this essential and uniquely human faculty is suspended along with all memory of what feeling, need or notion inspired the thing in the first place. To the extent that it is moulded and constrained by opinion polls and media spin, modern political language is the cousin of the managerial and just as alienating. To speak or be spoken to in either variety is to be 'not in this world'.

Bear in mind just the same that if we deface the War Memorial or rampage through St Paul's with a sledgehammer we will be locked up as criminals or lunatics. We can expect the same treatment if we release some noxious weed or insect into the natural environment. It is right that the culture and environment should be so respected. Yet every day we vandalise the language, which is the foundation, the frame and joinery of the culture, if not its greatest glory, and there is no penalty and no way to impose one. We can only be indignant. And we should resist.

> Wheresoever manners and fashions
> are corrupted, language is. It imitates
> the public riot.
> Ben Jonson

PARROTS, WHEN THEY ARE separated from their flocks, know by instinct that they must quickly join another one or they will make a meal for hawks. It is from this understanding that their mimetic skill derives. On finding any other horde they try to blend by mimicking its members. They do as the Romans do. If it is a Catholic household in which they find themselves, they might recite Hail Marys. Among blasphemers, they'll blaspheme. Where it is customary to curse the dog or tap the barometer, they curse the dog or tap the barometer. Whatever is most frequently repeated sounds to them definitive, and this is the one they imitate. Every day for forty years, regardless of the context, a bird might screech, 'Don't forget your hat!' or shout 'Oh What a Feeling!' all day long, much as advertisers do. Parrots never learn the language, but are smart enough to know, like people involved in marketing, that one or two catch phrases will satisfy most people.

Our language grows, mutates and ossifies in a similar way. We are all inclined to imitate the sounds we hear. Fashion dictates many words and phrases. In foreign countries we pick up accents and inflections. We tune ourselves to the cadences of unfamiliar dining rooms. Politicians go amongst the people primed with local knowledge and saying 'Gidday' or 'How do you do', according to the prevailing custom. Priests murmur Latin phrases that are full of meaning even to their non-Latin-speaking flocks. Street gangs, sports clubs, political parties, families, people who for all kinds of reasons are regularly together, naturally develop a vernacular as a kind of bonding and those who want to join must learn it. Ideologues speak in language best understood by ideologues of like mind: it is called 'preaching to the converted' and it is probably a species of narcissism, like a budgerigar talking to itself in a mirror.

Organisations frequently impose a language of a certain shape on members and employees. Military forces seem to have done it always, and now companies imitate the military example, and all kinds of other outfits imitate the companies. Politics got slogans from military battalions – the word 'slogan' comes from the Gaelic and literally means a battle cry. No sooner were there slogans in politics than there were also 'weasel words': sly words that do not mean what they appear to, or have an unseen purpose. To be involved with politics is to make a pact with the devil, Max Weber said. Should we then expect the language of politics to have something diabolical about it? And if politicians can't resist temptation, why should advertising and marketing? Why should companies? The company is a miracle of the modern world:

... the establishment of a comprehensive feedback process industry at the national, State / Territory, and regional levels to inform the continuous improvement of the Training Packages in future iterations ...
Australian Government

The soul was not made to dwell in a thing: and when forced to it, there is no part of that soul but suffers violence.
Simone Weil, 'The Iliad, Poem of Might'

in fact it is almost true to say that the limited liability company was the beginning of the modern age. The point at which the age becomes *post*modern is marked, perhaps, by companies taking their liability for the language to be limited.

The English language has always been prey to fashion, and on the evidence so far we should not fear for its survival. Fashions come and go, but the language moves on, taking with it whatever remains useful or interesting, discarding what is colourless or vain. The language has proved much stronger than any human attempt to contain it: Samuel Johnson and, on the other side of the Atlantic, Noah Webster, both tried to tie it down and both failed magnificently. Waves of grammarians have followed them. There have always been people to declare that this or that is the only definition of a word, and this is the only way to pronounce it; this is the only way to arrange a sentence and this the only way punctuate it. These people are essential, but only in the way that lifeboats are to an ocean liner.

The historical view suggests we can relax. English has survived everything that's been thrown at it: political and social revolution, industrial and technological revolutions, colonialism and post-colonialism, mass education, mass media, mass society. More than just surviving these upheavals, it adapts and grows, is strengthened and enriched by them. And never has it grown more than now: by one estimate, at the rate of more than 20,000 words a year, and for every new word several old ones change their meanings or sprout additional ones. It is wondrous on this level.

And yet, as it grows it is depleting. In the information age the public language is coming down to an ugly, sub-literate universal form with a fraction of the richness that living English has. Relative to the potential of language, the new form approximates a parrot's usage. It is cliché-ridden and lacks meaning, energy, imagery and rhythm. It also lacks words. It struggles to express the human. Buzz words abound in it. Platitudes iron it flat. The language is hostile to communion, which is the purpose of language. It cannot touch provenance. It stifles reason, imagination and the promise of truth. Look at a block of 1960s Housing Commission flats and you have the shape and dysfunction of it. Listen and you can hear the echoes of authoritarian cant. Our public language is becoming a non-language. Errors of grammar are irritating; slovenly, colloquial or hybrid speech can be gruesome; but English also gets much of its vigour and resilience from sponta-neous invention and the colonial cultural mix. Compared to the general malaise, even the language of the law is harmless and at least amuses those who practise it. These are to the language as a few biting insects are to the tsetse fly: as an itch is to a slow, sleeping death.

The cage fell off, the parrot took fright and cried out: 'Pre-sent arms!'
Turgenev, *Yakov Pasynkov*

'We are demotivated', said Sergeant Chris Grisham, a military intelligence officer.
News report from Iraq

There have been signs of decay in the language of politics and academia for years, but the direst symptoms are in business; and the curse has spread through the pursuit of business models in places that were never businesses. Universities that once valued and defended culture have swallowed the creed whole. Libraries, galleries and museums, banks and welfare agencies now parrot it. The public sector spouts it as loudly as the private does. It is the language of all levels of government including the very local. They speak of *focusing on the delivery of outputs* and matching decisions to *strategic initiatives*. Almost invariably these *strategic initiatives* are *key* strategic initiatives. In this language, schools, bank branches and libraries are closed down. In an education curriculum or the mission statement of an international fast food chain you will hear the same phrases. Military leaders while actually conducting wars sound like marketing gurus, and politicians sound like both of them. If one day in the finance pages you encounter *critical deliverables*, do not be surprised if it turns up the next day when you're listening to the football. The public language has all these variants and all of them are infected, if not dead. It is the grey death of the globalised world.

Those in the vanguard seem determined to create a new language for the new times they are bringing into being: new words to describe the new machinery, new words for the new processes, new words for leadership and management, new words to measure value and priority, new words to govern behaviour; slogans to live our lives by. Inevitably, those who follow the business model follow their lead in language: and while it is partly to imitate, to impress or to melt into the milieu, it is also because this is the language in which they are taught. It is part of the package.

In this revolution we are encouraged to take up the new, like those chimps who took up fire millions of years ago. We learn the laws of the free market as an earlier generation learned the laws of selection: that we must be competitive, that the adaptable survive and the rest are swallowed up. We are so thoroughly persuaded that everything depends on adapting to the new, we are letting go of the language for no better reason than that it is very old.

Consider these two sentences. They are not the worst specimens ever seen, but they are typical of the kind. The writer seeks applications for a job in marketing.

Due to the nature of our industry and also the breadth of our core business offering, we have a large list of blue chip clients. Cocky Marketing has a unique positioning in the Australian market place and intends to grow upon this in the coming years.

The successful applicant, the advertisement continues, will possess *an eye for detail, ability to multi-task, creativity, confident ability to communicate, amicable* (sic) *personality and ability to drive manual vehicle.* The language could lead us to wonder if the person advertising does not lack at least the first four skills. Yet the people who respond to the advertisement are not likely to notice any shortcomings. This kind of writing is now endemic: it is learned, practised, expected, demanded. It is writing of the kind George Orwell said was tacked together like the sections of a prefabricated henhouse.

Grammar is not the problem. To work on the grammar is like treating a man's dandruff when he has

---

A man may take to drink because he feels himself to be a failure, and then fail all the more completely because he drinks. It is rather the same thing that is happening to the English language. It becomes ugly and inaccurate because our thoughts are foolish, but the slovenliness of our language makes it easier for us to have foolish thoughts. The point is that the process is reversible. Modern English, especially written English, is full of bad habits which spread by imitation and which can be avoided if one is willing to take the necessary trouble. If one gets rid of these habits one can think more clearly, and to think clearly is a necessary first step toward political regeneration: so that the fight against bad English is not frivolous and is not the exclusive concern of professional writers.

George Orwell, *Politics and the English Language*

gangrene. The thing is systemically ill. It does not respond to any form of massage or manipulation. You try surgery and when you've finished there's more on the floor than on the table. Look again and you realise it has been a corpse all along. It is composed entirely of dead matter, except perhaps for the bit about the *blue chip clients*, whatever they are. Leave it at – *We have a large list of blue chip clients and* (if you must) *a unique position* (no *ing*) *in the Australian market place* – and this simple sentence looks almost heroic. It might be hogwash, but it's plainer hogwash and it doesn't turn to fog the instant it makes contact with a reader's brain.

You will see writing of this kind wherever the influence of marketing and managerialism has seeped, which is to say pretty well everywhere. It is the language of both private and public sectors, of McDonald's, your financial institution, your library, your local member, your national intelligence organisation. It comes through your door and down your phone: in letters from public utilities, government departments, local councils, your children's school, banks, insurance companies and telephone companies, all of them telling you that their main purpose is to *better address outcomes for all our customers to better achieve our goals*. It will be put before you in PowerPoint presentations; it will blurt across your computer screen – sometimes with a friend's name and email address at the bottom. Sometimes you will see that you have written it yourself. At any moment of the working day the screen might remind you that you are employed to *validate logic models for assigning accountabilities*. In hybrid forms, it issues from the mouths of commanders of armies and leaders of nations, as if to say that in our advanced societies, government and

And the Lord said, Behold, the people is one, and they have all one language; and this they begin to do: and now nothing will be restrained from them, which they have imagined to do.

Go to, let us go down, and there confound their language, that they may not understand one another's speech . . .

Genesis 11:6–9

Prefer geniality to grammar.

Henry Watson Fowler and Francis George Fowler, *The King's English*

war, like all other enterprises, come down to marketing or marketing *events*. We may be sure that in certain influential quarters there are people who believe that this is why we are so advanced.

This blurring of the corporate (or managerial) with more traditional (or primitive) human activity creates confusing environments for players. Just as a parrot might screech all day for half a century, 'Where's my other sock?', as if socks mattered to a bird, a politician will now talk about promises being *core* and *non-core* as if these business categories mattered to a promise. In the same way, teenage basketballers are told to be *accountable* as if they were global corporations. Footballers and cricketers are also told to be *accountable*, and in post-match interviews declare that because they were they won. So far no one has been heard to say that they played *transparent* football, but in May this year a South Australian football commentator told the listening public that *the bottom line* of entering the forward line was *validation by the leg*. And it probably is, *at the end of the day*.

It is likely that nothing attempted outside the corporate world can change what is happening to the language within it. The management revolution will continue, the corporation will continue to evolve and the language will evolve with it. The relationship is systemic. Management language has been changing ever since the first stage of the 'management revolution' in the 1930s when managers started to be more important than proprietors, control more important than ownership. Billy Wilder's 1960 film, *The Apartment*, was in part a satire on the command and control structure of management and the language that went with it. Company employee, Jack Lemmon, tacks *wise* on to every second word – *company-wise, control-wise, lending your apartment to your superiors to have affairs in-wise.* No one works or talks like that any more. They say *in respect of*, *in regard to*, and *in terms of*.

The change is foreseen in another masterpiece of those years, Vladimir Nabokov's *Lolita*. The principal of Lolita's school tells Humbert Humbert:

. . . we are more interested in communication than composition. That is, with due respect to Shakespeare and others, we want our girls to *communicate* freely with the live world around them rather than plunge into musty old books . . .We think, Dr Humbert, in organismal and organisational terms . . . What do we mean by education? . . . we live not only in a world of thoughts but a world of things . . . Words without experience are meaningless.

While most discussions of knowledge management have treated commitment as a binary variable, underlying theory suggests otherwise. Commitment can be better represented in terms of a continuum ranging from negligible or partial commitment to the KMS, and from avoidance (non use) to meagre and unenthusiastic use (compliant use) to skilled, enthusiastic and consistent use (committed use) of the KMS).

Yogesh Malholtra *(Syracuse University of Management)* and Dennis F. Galletta *(Joseph M. Kratz Graduate School of Business)* 'Role of Commitment and Motivation in Knowledge Management Systems Implementation: Theory, Conceptualisation, and Measurement of Antecedents of Success'

The Principal's principles are those of the modern manager and communications teacher. He wanted to leave out of Lolita's education what they leave out: namely, the human mind – the thing that arrives at meaning through language and will not, without coercion or deceit, reduce to a cog in a machine or an item of organisation. Nabokov's Principal has triumphed absolutely.

In today's *leading edge* companies, *networks* have replaced the vertical hierarchies of forty years ago; directives have given way to *communications* within and between the *networks*. This new model, we are told, makes for much faster decision-making, essential in modern global companies built around products, customers and geography: so much faster that managers are *nodes*. *Communications* bounce off these nodes in *horizontal flows* across *silos*. Nodes are 'what it is all about', the experts say: *nodes* and *networking between silos*. The essential difference between *leading edge* companies now, and companies in the days of *The Apartment*, is that in the old days only the top end of the hierarchy had daily need of communicating: now, just about everyone in the company does. In the company, as at Lolita's school, people do not talk about language, or English or grammar or expression – they talk about *Communications*.

This is a radical change. The new model, a McKinsey's heavyweight tells us, 'should liberate the company from the past'. Certainly it liberates the company from the language of the past, which means a lot of people are liberated from the language of their parents; much as the inhabitants of Babel were liberated by God when He confounded them. Judging an employee's performance, for example, comes down to this:

The role of the corporate centre is to worry about talent and how people do relative to each other. Workers build a set of intangibles around who they are. If they are not appreciated for their value-added they will go somewhere else.

Ask yourself: would you stay if your *value-added* was not appreciated?

The global company is the spearhead and exemplar of management change. We can presume that it will become, if it is not already, the *paradigm*, *the benchmark*, *world's best practice*, the *KPI (key performance indicator)* of all KPIs; which means within a year or two your football club will imitate it, as presently they imitate the fashion for *paradigms*, *benchmarks*, *KPIs* and (seriously, they have been heard to say it) *best practice*. It's all fashion, of course, and fashion is imitation. Wherever modern management goes, however, the fashion for networking makes imitation

Once on paper, words assume a horrifying concreteness. All the beautiful fluidity of thought is gone, replaced by rows of squalid and humourless squiggles. Yet these squiggles (this is the horrifying part) have somehow become 'your idea' . . . 'If you want your idea to get better', they seem to say, 'you will have to deal with us.' But you are already realising as you stare at them, that your idea is utterly vapid — and you haven't even had it yet.

Louis Menand,
New Yorker

compulsory. Communication is the primary purpose of the networks. Everyone in the networks communicates in the same language, everyone thinks in it, and no one, it seems, thinks about anything else: except of course if their *value-added* has been noticed relative to other network members, which does make it possible that business is not the only thing going on in these *silos*. A little ambition, a little envy, a little of the kind of thing that went on in the dark ages of *The Apartment*. We can hope.

Schools of communications have appeared all over the globe and manuals of communication skills proliferate to feed them. Some of these manuals make the point that people teaching communications are often the hardest people on earth to understand, that schools of communications are the worst places for jargon. The better manuals are models of clarity, and clarity is what they want their readers to achieve. They stress short sentences, the active voice, nouns and verbs without adjectives and adverbs fending for them: simplicity, directness. Jargon they properly despise. Structuralism, poststructuralism, postmodernism and other fashionable academic theories are put to the torch; along with similes, metaphors and figures of speech in general. (There goes the torch.)

Comfortingly Orwellian as this may sound, it is also a bit silly. If theory is incomprehensible it is useless: and, if it defies comprehension, a description of a sunset or a centaur is also useless. True, theory is more likely to be incomprehensible than description, but much theory is more useful and stimulating. For instance, it can help us see that if latter day Orwellians think language is just a matter of matching the right words to the right things, they are wrong. At best the idea represents a worthy ambition: at worst it's as fanciful as any 'theory' ever was, and a doctrine to rob language of its subtle powers and splendour. To teach the doctrine robs students as well. It is one thing to feed them only chops: much worse to tell them that chops are all a lamb comprises.

It is true, the communications teachers say, that the admirable Shakespeare used figures of speech: 'In Shakespeare's time, however, language of this kind was common to everyday speech, and thus natural to the period.' And sure enough, you open Francis Bacon, who lived in Shakespeare's time, and at once we find him saying that a wrong done out of ill-nature is 'like the thorn or briar, which prick and scratch'; and just a couple of lines on, 'cowards are like the arrow that flieth in the dark'. These days, say the communications writers, we don't talk or write like this. We talk plainly, or aspire to do so. Rarely as plainly as Bacon, however. Bacon, 'the first that writ our language correctly', was for the most part a plain writer. Shakespeare was colourful, Bacon was plain. It seems after all there was no one way to write in the seventeenth century. And in truth there never has been.

On balance, the influence of these communications manuals is likely to be good – at least for communications. The best kind of writing, they suggest, is writing we don't notice (and how pleasant it would be not to notice much of the writing one has to read). To communicate by writing – or by public speaking – is to convey information accurately and precisely. It is the effect of the information that matters, not the effect of the words. After all, this is an information society, not a word society. No doubt when the information in the information society becomes more stimulating, it will be heaven. In the meantime, the utilitarian doctrine propounded in communications manuals does not offer a lot for our enjoyment.

Clarity and precision are highly desirable in language, and much more enjoyable than dullness and prolixity. But language is capable of expressing more than information: it is a vehicle of the imagination

There is a weird power in a spoken word . . . And a word carries far – very far – deals destruction through time as the bullets go flying through space.

Joseph Conrad,
Lord Jim

Words ought to be a little wild for they are the assault of thoughts on the unthinking.

J.M. Keynes

Information can tell us everything. It has all the answers.
But they are answers to questions we have not asked, and which doubtless don't even arise.

Jean Baudrillard,
Cool Memories

and the emotions. 'We make all our relationships by talk, all our institutions, all our roles,' as Greg Dening says. We do not make them with information alone. We use words not only to describe what we know, but sometimes also to discover what we don't know. No one would recommend a manual of communications that dealt mainly in figures of speech or 'flowery words'. Equally, no one with a care for the language can recommend improving it by proscribing all adornment and adventure and closing off half its possibilities. No one with a care for people, either, and no one who believes that information need not define all of life in the information age.

One day perhaps someone will be interested enough to trace the point at which this journey into fog began. Was it the Chicago School of economics? When supply-side economics became the main game of politics? Was it the management revolution? Microsoft? (No one *enhances* like the IT business.) Or when Labor parties stopped pretending to be socialist and gave up the fight against the corporation? Whatever it was, the overlap between political and business language became a merger in the early 1980s when economics (and business) became so decidedly the main game. In the years since then business language has been steadily degenerating, mauled by the new religions of technology and management. But its range now spreads well beyond politics and the corporations, and into all the corners of our lives. The same depleted and impenetrable sludge is taught in schools of marketing and business. And, significantly, it is taught in groups; in conscious or unconscious anticipation of the 'teams' that corporate management favours. Few teaching strategies could do

Lolita, light of my
life, fire of my loins.
My sin, my soul.
Lo-lee-ta: the tip of
the tongue taking a
trip of three steps
down the palate to
tap, at three, on the
teeth. Lo. Lee. Ta.
Vladimir Nabokov, *Lolita*

He had only one
interpretation of
history and politics,
an economic one; he
saw in altruism the
perspicacious self-
interest of cunning
ambition . . .
   He had a
vocabulary just
adapted to his needs,
disliked slang and
commonplaces but
misunderstood a
good many ordinary
words and elided
more sounds in
speaking than
anyone else in Paris.
Christina Stead,
House of all Nations

more to discourage fluency or independent thought. Combine it with the requirement that every 'thought' comes with a reference to some authority, when every authority is written to the same formula and in the same style, and you have guaranteed copious muck, ad nauseam. Put another way, you have doctrine, doctrinally taught.

If in your professional life you want to understand your fellow human beings and be understood by them, practise with a mission statement. And remember, everything worth putting on paper, slide or disk has a dot in front of it. It should look something like this:

<u>What We Stand For</u>: *Our Core Beliefs and Values*

- *Objectivity is the substance of intelligence, a deep commitment to the customer in its forms and timing.*

Don't worry if you're not entirely sure what this means. Once you have mastered the style you are half way to the philosophy, which is why the easiest way to write a mission statement is to borrow someone else's. Any sort of outfit will do: a supermarket chain, a public service department or an intelligence organisation. The one quoted here is the CIA's. The dot point preceding the previous one is:

- *Intelligence that adds substantial value to the management of crises, the conduct of war, and the development of policy.*

If you continue to use the CIA model – but McDonald's will do just as well – mention, like they do, *accountability, teamwork, commitment, continuous improvement* and *adapting to evolving customer needs*. Friends, Romans, customers . . . Of the customer, by the customer, for the customer shall not perish from the earth.

When I told the telecommunications company, Optus, that I was transferring my accounts to its rival, Telstra, a reply came addressed *Dear Valued Customer*. They asked me to *accept our sincerest apologies for any inconvenience or frustration the billing issue, raised may have caused. Optus constantly strives to give our customer's* (sic) *our best service experience and it is of some concern to us to hear that your expectations were not met by Optus in this instance.*

It is not the misplaced comma and apostrophe that kills these sentences. It's the *billing issue, service experience*; and the glue in the next sentence: *constantly strives, some concern to us, in this instance*. The aim is to sound polite and helpful, but the result is unctuous, unhelpful and depressing. You cannot get through such prose. And subliminally at least, that is the bigger message: you cannot

As long as we live, and whatever fate may have been assigned to us, or we have chosen, there is no doubt that the better the quality of our communication, the more useful (and agreeable) to ourselves and others we will be and the longer we will be remembered. He who does not know how to communicate, or communicates badly, in a code that belongs only to him or a few others, is unhappy, and spreads unhappiness around him. If he communicates badly deliberately, he is wicked or at least a discourteous person, because he imposes labour, anguish, or boredom on his readers.

Primo Levi,
On Obscure Writing

succeed in this. Submit. Roll over. The language of corporations is like a vampire without fangs; it has no venom or bite but you don't want it hanging off your neck just the same.

Modern public language hand-cuffs words to action, ideas to matter, the pure thought to the dirty deed. It collapses the categories for the sake of convenience. What you think and what you are become one, which is the *team*, where every-one has learned to think the same thoughts, or at least within the same *parameters*. If these para-meters are defined by what is called *Knowledge Management* (KM) very likely they encompass a *knowledge entity*. *Knowledge entities are incomplete if they do not cultivate a dialog* (sic) *between the members of the community of practice to advance the defining and refining of a socially constructed process.* *Knowledge Management* is one more mutant form of the managerialism that walks blithely over a whole tradition of Western philosophy, crushing all subtleties and distinctions.

Verbs are ground out of exis-tence, nouns driven into service as a substitute for them; all but a few adjectives (*robust, vibrant, enhanced*) are abandoned along with metaphors because they are untidy distractions from the main objective, which is a serviceable instrument of communication. 'First the adjectives wither, then the verbs', Elias Canetti said.

All elegance and gravity has gone from public language, and all its light-footed potential to intrigue, delight and stimulate our hearts and minds. We use language to deal with our moral and political dilemmas, but not this language. This language is not capable of serious deliberation. It could no more carry a complex argument than it could describe the sound of a nightingale. Listen to it in the political and corporate landscape and you hear noises that our recent ancestors might have taken for Gaelic or Swahili, and we ourselves do not always understand. Even some of those who speak and write it will tell you that they don't know quite what it means. Then again, they do not exactly speak or write so much as *implement* it.

The public realm has been in decline since governments retreated from the economy and private companies moved in to take their place. The operation extends well beyond privatised public utilities in gas, water, electricity and transport. Economic revolution has transformed our institutions – colleges and universities, hospitals and medical practices, the public service itself – and transformed our relationships with them in doing so. As the private sector has replaced the public it has found itself obliged to pick up functions and responsibilities that had belonged to governments. They pick them up in different ways, and they use a different term for them: they call it *investing in social capital.* Indeed, they use a very different language. The old bureaucratic – *yours of the 4th inst.* – forms were pompous, obscure and prolix. Sir Ernest Gowers' *Plain Words*, Fowler's *Modern English Usage*, and centuries of satire were necessary to decode and knock the stuffing out of them. But at least there was stuffing to be knocked. Generally there was a meaning to be reached, something to be saved. And there was room in this official language for elegant exceptions, a drollery, a little tartness, sudden and unexpected flair. I know people who while working in the old bureaucracies read much of the literary canon, including Joyce and Kafka, in their spare time. No one can prove that this was not public time and money well spent.

Of course the new regimes will never allow the same chance to employees. James and J.S. Mill wrote books that changed the course of history while working for the East India Company, a multinational. Not today they wouldn't. Today they would be attending countless meetings, seminars and

I am delighted to be able to share with you some important news about our company. On 1 July we will be changing our name to Asteron. The name Asteron is coined from the Greek work 'astron', which means star. Throughout history stars have been recognised as icons that represent navigation, distinction and excellence and as such the star theme is truly representative of Asteron's mission and organisational values.

Letter from insurance company

conferences to update their knowledge of work-related subjects, all of them conducted in the mind-maiming language of managerialism. And, to draw a longer bow, the more of these *fora* (*fora*, archaic plural of forum, now common in up-to-date bureaucracies and NGOs where they attend a lot of forums. *In my role as chairperson last year I attended several international <u>fora</u>*) people spend time in, the less likely it is that they will ever know the comfort of seeing their lives reflected in Joseph K or Leopold Bloom or Mr Casaubon. And the benefits of such self-knowledge and of exposure to good writing will, it follows, never find a way into their language.

That is the dire point. Bad as the old language could be, there were always cracks in it and comprehensible, even creative, language could sometimes squeeze through. And even the worst of it was always at least a variant or mutation of the language we all understood. But great lumps of the new language are unrelated to anything ever spoken. It's a kind of self-sealing grout that keeps its speakers – and meaning – unconnected and unexposed to ordinary thought and feeling: *As part of the electronic delivery strategy the vision to enable customers to transact low face value commoditised financial market instruments electronically and seamlessly.* Probably this means that customers will be able to transfer money by electronic means for a reasonable price, but who can say? It might be a secret message that only their customers understand.

The meaning aside, the sentence just quoted contains a common manoeuvre in corporate language: so common, if reason didn't tell us otherwise we might

Puffing Billy is strategically important as it is one of the region's most significant drawcards. The railway has a very high visitor recognition, and is one of the key 'attractors' that drives visitation to the region . . . The Facilities Enhancement Project aims to maintain and further develop the facilities and services of the Puffing Billy railway as a significant world-class tourist attraction in the lead-up to the Commonwealth Games. It focuses on the high priority capital works identified in the ETRB strategic plan.

Victorian Government

conclude it bears some connection to the way organisations actually think and act. The manoeuvre is with the word *strategy*. *The electronic delivery strategy makes it possible to deliver things electronically.* This is very much as we would expect: imagine our surprise if the strategy brought about seamless delivery by rowboat. We might put it down to careless repetition if the same *strategy* did not turn up in so many annual reports, mission statements, even applications for academic research. All modern organisations (and many modern organised people no doubt) must regularly (if not continuously, in the interests of *continuous improvement*) measure their performance. This is done with *KPIs*. *KPIs* are to modern managers what the stars were to early navigation. They set their course by strategic goals and mark them off against results. Who knows, the method may do wonders for the bottom line and human happiness, but you would not think so from what shows on the page. On the page it has a crude pedagogical quality, as if designed for remedial high school students.

Under a general heading of, say, *Leadership*, we see columns and dot points. One column is headed *Strategies* and the other *Results*. Under *Leadership* we get windy summaries of ambitions. The following is typical: *The Museum will be recognised locally, nationally or internationally as an industry* (sic) *leader through the exemplary way it conducts its activities, serves the community, is accountable to government and responds to sponsors' needs*. Under *Strategies* we read: *Through a collaborative and inclusive process, develop strategic support for regional museums throughout the State*. And in the next column under *Results*: *The Committee facilitated discussions about strategies for effective collaboration and support for regional touring exhibitions*.

There are dozens of strategies and for each of them results must be found. It is no surprise that sometimes the two seem to be all but interchangeable, and there is little to persuade us that in every case the results are written in the light of the *strategy* and not the other way round. The result is something that, for all the talk of *key outputs* (read exhibitions and research) and being *a preferred provider of enjoyable and educational experiences* (visits and tours), looks less like an analysis than blarney, or a charmless parody of Soviet bureaucracy.

What you don't sound like is a museum, a research institution, an institution of character. You say you want to be a *world player* (one state library says *world* three times in its mission statement, though it's not sure what to call the people, formerly known as 'readers', who use the library), but you must also be *community and customer focused*. Whatever your business – brain research, rabbit trapping, underwear manufacturing – you must be equal to the *world's best practice*, and *responsive to customer needs*, *strategic* (of course) and *accountable*, and so on. So you must also be prolix and utterly predictable. You are trapped in the language like a parrot in a cage.

I can think of no better demonstration of the syndrome than when, a few years ago, a Premier of Victoria stood on a stage in front of a troupe of modern dancers who had just completed a performance. The speech began with an appreciation of the dancers' art, but soon veered towards something like he might have delivered in a car plant at the launch of a new model, or to a press conference on Budget night. It was a speech of the kind Australian politicians had been giving for a decade – ever since we learned the trade balance was awry and we must change or follow Argentina to the economic graveyard. Most of the good old lines were there: I seem to remember *international best practice* even found a way into it. I also remember the dance troupe

Mother fled, screaming. She ran inside and called the children. Sal assisted her. They trooped in like wallabies, all but Joe. He was away earning money. He was getting a shilling a week from Maloney for chasing cockatoos from the corn.

Steele Rudd,
On Our Selection

The word is the Verb, and the Verb is God.

Victor Hugo,
Contemplations

whose presence on the stage was taken to justify the Premier's theme. Because recently they had been induced to leave Sydney and make their home in Melbourne, much as the Formula One Grand Prix had been snatched from Adelaide, they were proof of dynamic market forces. That a good part of their act satirised these forces was immaterial. They were good; they had been well-reviewed in Europe, hence the talk about competitiveness. So the usual mantras had been rolled out, and the chance of spontaneity reined in. But the dancers' proof of their international competitiveness had left them in a muck sweat, detumescing and blowing like horses after a race, three-quarters naked, pulsing. It was, as they so often say in the arts, and many other places nowadays, *in terms of* an evening in the theatre, quite bizarre.

In terms of is to the language what a codling moth is to an apple tree and just as exasperating. For instance: *Both oil and high tech sectors are characterised by 'leader' and 'laggard' companies in terms of environmental performance.* And all sectors are characterised by dead words. What need, except the need of habit or the need to sound like everyone else in the consultancy sector, is satisfied by *in terms of* in this sentence? For that matter, what good does *characterised* do? Or *environmental performance*? Couldn't they just say: *in both sectors there are companies that lead on the environment and companies that lag behind*?

Here we go again: . . . *the US was an early leader in the area of information disclosure and, in terms of government information, remains far more transparent than many European countries.* We are so used to the expression we may not notice it at first. But look again and you see it has

'You can make a
gigantic difference
simply by buying
products with the
Australian Made
logo on them.'
Tim Fischer

How forcible are
right words!
Job 6:25

We are like the exile
in a foreign land
whose own language
shrinks while he
parrots the same
constantly familiar
phrases of the one
that surrounds him.
Jean Amery,
'How Much Home Does a
Person Need?'

a grub in it. Remove the grub and you have: *the US was an early leader in the area of information disclosure and government information remains far more transparent than many European countries*. This is not precisely what you want, but once you've made the first move you can see the others, at least as far as saying, *and US governments are still far more transparent than many European countries*. Who knows, you may decide that *transparent* is vague and *area* is a waste of space. So you might re-write the sentence as: . . . *the US was an early leader in information disclosure and US governments continue to disclose much more than many European countries*. You might prefer *disclosing information* to *information disclosure*. You might decide the bit about being an *early leader* is not worth the trouble. You might want to adjust the nuances, but now at least there are nuances to adjust.

Corporate leaders sometimes have good reason to twist their language into knots and obscure the meaning of it, but more often it is simply habit. They have forgotten the other way of speaking: the one in which you try to say what you mean. Instead they welcome their audience and proceed immediately to put them in a coma by announcing their intention to spend the next half hour *outlining the company's key strategies and initiatives going forward*, and their *commitment* to fill *capability gaps* and *enhance sustainable growth for the benefit of all stakeholders*.

But habit is not the only thing that motivates them. They suffer from the same pomposity that afflicts most people when they write formally or make formal speeches. That may be letting many of them off too lightly: some are pompous because it's their nature to be and no one has ever told them it's unattractive – to read, hear and watch. It is the verbal equivalent of wearing epaulettes and braid, or a hat with bones and feathers in it: or, because pomposity is sometimes defensive, a flak jacket. Even when it is used as a shield against uncertainty, pompous language is a weapon, an expression of power. Part of it is a mistaken effort to elevate the tone. Pomposity assumes that she who elevates the tone will herself be elevated. Even beyond scrutiny. The risk, which the truly pompous never see, is that an opposite effect is achieved or the tone moves sideways into unselfconscious parody. Not that everyone will laugh when they encounter this, an example from the public sector:

Unfortunately, due to the recent unprecedented demand for the publication Australian Meteorological Radio Facsimile Broadcasts, and therefore a diminution of stocks, there is now an exigency to restrict dissemination of this publication to professional end-users and institutions only.

Speakers and writers may also think it useful to keep their audience so deep in darkness they will not be able to see the flaws or conclude they must be stupid not to understand. Academics, teachers and priests are likely to recognise the same conceit in their professions. To the extent that all public performance is an effort to narrow the focus of an audience on to a single point of light – from whence comes the voice of truth – probably there is always a temptation to make words arcane, magical and (why not?) incomprehensible. Perhaps they talk about *maximising synergies* and *pushing the envelope* to satisfy some ancient urge.

Keen to demonstrate that they are competitive, internationally benchmarked sorts of outfits, corporations and government departments write to advise their customers they have thought of ways to serve us better. A letter came last year announcing *some enhancements to our billing systems to serve* you *better*. It continued: *These recent enhancements to our billing systems may mean you receive your next bill later*

'The commitment to Australia is the one thing needed to be a true Australian.'
Bob Hawke

They said, 'You
   have a blue guitar,
You do not play
   things as they are.'
The man replied,
   'Things as they are
Are changed upon
   the blue guitar.'
Wallace Stevens

than usual, and you may also notice some minor format changes. All normal payment terms and conditions still apply. Nothing else in the letter explained what the *enhancements* were, but that is the way with *enhancements* – often they don't amount to anything at all. It's just that the word *enhancement* has become irresistible like ice cream or chicken pox. *Enhance* is the McDonald's of corporate English. The letter went on:

At Optus we are paving the way for better, more enhanced ways of doing business, and these enhanced systems are designed to deliver on that commitment. These improvements will allow for more flexible and efficient billing options as we move forward.

This is a clag sandwich with the lot; old clichés and clichés recently coined. We begin by *paving the way* and then we get *enhanced* (and more *enhanced* – four *enhances* in fifty words), and *commitment* on which we *deliver*, and *flexible* and *efficient* and *options*, and it is all done, of course, as we *move forward*. Government documents and company annual reports of more than two pages will almost always contain these last two words. The same is true of party statements, mission statements, consultancy reports and annual reports.

Commitment is the worst kind of politician's word. To say they are *committed* to something does not mean they believe it (If they did, why not say so?); or that they will do it (If they will, why not do so?). It is a standard weasel word, a weed which spread with the fashion for mission statements, new management theories and sports psychology. There is deceit, including self-deceit, at its

ABSTRACTITIS.
The effect of this
disease, now
endemic on both
sides of the Atlantic,
is to make the
patient write such
sentences as
*Participation by the men in
the control of the industry
is non-existent* instead
of *The men have no part
in the control of the
industry*.
H.W. Fowler, *Modern
English Usage*

'They risk-taked all
day.'
AFL Coach

heart; but, as with all weeds, *com-mitment*'s main offence is to the landscape. It is the ugliness of it and the ubiquity. It might not fool us, but it does depress us.

Enhance can mean anything, which is why it's so popular with people who have lost the ability to say what they mean. Once we might have said *improve*, or *augment*, or *illuminate*, or *accelerate*, or *lengthen*, *broaden* or make *hairier* – any one of hundreds of verbs. Now we say 'enhance'. We enhance our competitiveness, our hair colour, our national security, our breasts, our chances and our billing systems. We enhance our defence forces and our education. John Howard said the republic would not 'enhance' our independence. We *enhance* our *commitment* and we are *committed to enhancement*. We enhance our children's genes: or very soon some among us will, and it's a fair bet that many who choose the path of *genetic enhancement* will have *enhanced* much else in their lives beforehand. Their computers, their kitchens, their education, their lifestyles – they may even own one of those coffee makers that boasts a *froth enhancer*. Chances are they will see life as a succession of *enhancements*; and viewed from their particular balconies those *enhancements* will be looking very much like evidence of *continuous improvement*. It's uncanny how they coincide . . . like revealed truth, like a kind of miracle. So why wouldn't you *enhance* your kid? This language really works!

It is horrible and the more horribly familiar because the language of modern business is so like the language of modern politics. This, for instance, from the Hawke government:

Negotiation and persuasion are just as important in maintaining agreement and focus for the significant reforms which we have reached agreement about. The Government has worked hard to cement in place the negotiated settlements it has achieved. Agreement is the easy part! Implementation takes time.

An unmistakable symptom of the modern sludge is the *buzz word*. The thing about a buzz word is that, as a word, it doesn't buzz. It might *create* a buzz, but only under certain conditions. It might buzz in the reaches of the human mind and human culture that explain the preeminence of commerce, technology and politics in the world's affairs – but it doesn't buzz in a sentence.

Consider the buzz word *flexibility*. In another letter to me, a *valued customer*, Optus offered me a plan to provide the *flexibility to choose what best suits your needs*. When you think about it – which is not something this kind of language encourages – you see that, even if I needed flexibility, the sentence does not. It weighs the

As the sun sprang
up, leaving the
brilliant waters in
its wake,
climbing the bronze
sky to shower light
on immortal gods
and mortal men
across the
plowlands ripe
with grain –
the ship pulled into
Pylos, Neleus'
storied citadel,
where the people
lined the beaches,
sacrificing sleek
black bulls to
Poseidon,
god of the sea-blue
mane who shakes
the earth.

Homer, *The Odyssey*
(Translated by
Robert Fagles)

sentence down, and what's more distracts the reader from the very thing it wants him to recognise – that he can choose. Instead of offering him something he can do, it offers him something he can have, *flexibility*. Why not write: 'our plan allows you to choose'? Or: 'with our plan you can choose'? The noun inserts itself because somewhere in the writer's mind there is a jargon-seeking impulse that insists on inserting a *key* word, the buzz word. *Flexibility* will be there even if it kills the sentence stone-dead. *Flexibility* has been, if you like, *prioritised*. It has been deemed more important than the sentence itself.

It all began when companies got in their heads that it was necessary to be *flexible*. It goes with supply-side economics. It also goes with globalisation: with being *internationally competitive*. *Flexibility* has come to mean many things: production should be *flexible* – goods should be produced and delivered 'just in time', not en masse with rigid production lines and costly warehousing; management should be *flexible* – they should

41

think outside the square; and staff should be *flexible* – they should be multi-skilled and prepared to work hours that are *flexible*.

Governments also took up the *flexible* thing. Deregulation and a floating currency removed certain rigidities and the economy became more *flexible*. Soon it became obvious that the labour market would also have to become more *flexible*, so the trade unions were branded obsolescent unless they were *flexible*, and *flexible* enterprise agreements replaced *inflexible* awards. To meet the demands of the more *flexible* economy, universities and colleges became more *flexible* and rigidly opposed to anything that wasn't. The technological revolution became an information revolution, and both *enhanced* the *flexibility* of *consumer choice*. *Flexibility* is not only a pre-condition of success in the postmodern age, it now is also purported to describe it. The whole world, at least the affluent parts of it, which is to say the *flexible* parts, is *flexible*.

Some may think *enhanced* consumer choice has not *enhanced* existence much, or cast much light upon its meaning; and some will say that, like other fads and religions, choice has confined life more than it has widened it. Others will tell you that they have never spent more on telephony since it became a commercial contest. And even those who believe the whole enterprise in telecommunication has been one of history's great *enhancers* have to concede, whatever it has done for *flexibility*, it's done nothing for the language. It seems that consumer choice expands in inverse proportion to our vocabulary. We use fewer words and words of less variety. We arrange them with less imagination and dexterity. We tangle and abuse them. We take the richest soil the culture has and turn it into a few clods. Ever since Alexander Pope and Samuel Johnson took it upon themselves to eliminate the vulgar from the English tongue the language has been lopped at by snobs, pedants and prudes; but nothing done to it by the Augustans or the Victorians comes close to the violence of the managerial age. It is not the worst thing that can happen to people, but it cannot be described as progress.

The buzz word is the corporate equivalent of the political 'grab': the 'message' inserted by politicians in a speech or at a doorstop interview regardless of the subject, the context or the questions they are asked. Savvy political advisers arm their bloke with the word or phrase and he utters it come what may. Opening a new nursing home, he finds some laboured pretext in the speech to say that the political *Opposition are committed to decimating* (sic) *Australian families*. At the doorstop the journalists will say the war seems to be going badly and he will say that this is mere conjecture, but there is no doubting the Opposition's determination *to decimate Australian families*. Then they'll ask if interest rates are going to rise and he will say that that is a hypothetical question and he will not answer it, but there is nothing hypothetical about the Opposition's determination *to decimate Australian families*. They will ask about his recent meeting with Her Majesty and he will say, very well indeed, but while he is carrying on these essential and historic affairs of state Opposition members can think of nothing better than the *decimation of Australian families*. A news conference is always partly a contest to determine the day's story, and it's a contest politicians need to win: just as business needs to win the contest for our custom with advertising slogans. But, whoever wins, only rarely are we much enlightened by it.

Writing and painting both are forms of expression that depend on observation, imagination and skill, so what is said about one can sometimes also be said about the other. Not always, however: and because there is no one way to write or to paint, there are no rules applying to both. As most of us can enjoy equally, say, a Velasquez and a Picasso – or a watercolour and an oil – so we might like both plain prose and prose full of imagery:

> In Theodora's world a wet finger could have pressed the cardboard church, and pressed, until the smoking sky showed through. Sometimes an iron tram careered quite dangerously along the spine of a hill. People mopping their heads wondered uneasily into what they sank in Theodora Goodman's eyes. People casually looking were sucked in by some disturbance that was dark and strange.

'As we know, there are no known knowns. There are things we know we know. We also know there are known unknowns. That is to say we know there are some things we do not know. But there are also unknown unknowns, the ones we don't know we don't know.'

Donald Rumsfeld

I repeated, 'I shall not die, for I have not sinned against the light, I have not sinned against the light.' I never have been able quite to make out what I meant.

John Henry Newman,
Apologia Pro Vita Sua

As a model for public language, we might prefer Orwell to Patrick White, but not if his style is taken as encouragement for government and corporate writers to stick to the familiar and stay *on message*. The injunction 'write plainly' can be taken to mean 'write lifelessly'. To write clearly is not to think shallowly. It can be useful to pare away extraneous words and eschew the flourish in the interests of clarity, but there must be something at the end of it, at least something with a point.

There is a lesson for writing in what Delacroix said about his own favourite artist, Titian: he was 'the least mannered and therefore the most varied of painters . . . he constantly defers to genuine emotion. He has to render that emotion. Embellishment and a vain show of facility do not interest him. On the contrary he disdains everything that does not lead him to a livelier expression of his thought.' It is unlikely that a better general rule for writing was ever conceived.

Early signs that the rule is untaught or in eclipse include the absence of any signs of human sympathy in public language; or, worse, evidence that we have lost the forms of their expression. It was not unknown a while ago for officials to conclude their letters by wishing unsuccessful applicants and the like, 'good luck'; by 'hoping' (not *hopefully*) they would meet success, and 'thank you for applying'. I saw these sorts of words a few years ago in a letter from a Dublin office, and the feelings of lightness and good will they inspired were remarkable. It should not be difficult to reinstate such simple civilities, but half a generation of deadly decline would first have to be unlearned.

There might even be a clue in the changing style of music and other popular entertainments and rituals. When people write: *It is a self-regulatory agreement between the packaging chain and spheres of government, based on the principles of shared responsibility through product stewardship, and applied through the packaging chain, from raw materials to retailers, and the ultimate disposal of waste packaging*, it could be that they echo the structure of minds fashioned by din, chaos and method acting. The difference between this and a coherent sentence is perhaps the difference between Humphrey Bogart and Al Pacino, Cary Grant and Hugh Grant. It's the language of twitching narcissism derived more from imitation than from art.

What we can be sure of is that once this kind of language gets inside a company it spreads like duckweed down every channel of communication. Both private and public sector employees will tell you they write like this because the boss does, or because everyone else does. And because corporate and government speeches and policies are often composed by teams, or by chains stretching from a department, to an office, to a leader; and nowhere on the chain or in the team is there someone with the duty to think deeply or imaginatively about the subject, and write thoughtfully and imaginatively about it, the speeches and policies are indeed nailed together in prefabricated bits like one of Orwell's henhouses, and come out as witless and unfathomable dreck. And writers down the chain will tell you that when they write in plainer or richer English, higher authorities rewrite it in the house (read *global*) style.

Of course, it can't be entirely explained as mass submission to the power of a consuming fashion; much less to psychological or anthropological forces. It is an epidemic, but one in which, surely, some choice remains. Businesses can be forgiven their neologisms, but not their *technocratic* sludge. If they can find the means to *downsize*, *prioritise* and *implement quality function deployment* they can find better words for it.

Their failure becomes most acute when they try to bend the language into an instrument of

These reviews will be important inputs to future government action, including our assessment of the need to take action to increase baseload. However, that is not to say that in the meantime we are going to just sit on our hands.

Victorian Government

'Well that's odd . . . I've just robbed a man of his livelihood, and yet I feel strangely empty. Tell you what Smithers — have him beaten to a pulp.'

Montgomery Burns,
'The Simpsons'

persuasion. The fact is, of course, it can't be bent. It is incapable of carrying mood or emotion. It can neither admonish nor praise.

When, for example, those who speak the new language wish to demonstrate their concern for the less fortunate or the less profitable, or the community at large, they speak of addressing *the triple bottom line through corporate social responsibility* known as *CSR*. There is nothing wrong with this idea: rich private individuals and enlightened companies have been in the business of benefactions for a very long time. Some have done it in a spirit of charity and some have mixed charitable feelings with self-interest and as much good has come of it. Great and lasting good works have been done in this way: from mighty endowments to the arts and science of incalculable value to humankind, to the socks provided by the local haberdasher for a country football team. Some businesses offered their employees shares in the company and a voice in the management a century ago. Some were offering pensions, child-care and training on the job. Some took care of the environment. But today the corporations, having found it is good business to be good citizens, struggle to find words to describe their good intentions. Principally this is because their language has been stripped of meaning. They don't have words like *generous*, *charitable*, *kind*, and *share*; phrases like *give and take* or *enlightened self-interest*; or even words that governments and their bureaucracies, whose roles they are usurping, once used freely – *welfare*, *wealth transfer*, *social service*, *social benefit*, *social policy*, *social contract*. They would no more use words like these than they would use a word like 'greed'. They search for human

All animals are equal
but some animals are
more equal than
others.

George Orwell,
Animal Farm

He was apparently
a foreigner, for he
bore in his lapel a
green immigrant tag
reading 'Ellis Island
– Rush.' His clothes
were flapping hand-
me-downs greasy
with travel, and
altogether, he was
as extraordinary an
unhung horse-thief
as you would
encounter outside a
gypsy encampment.

S. J. Perelman

signs in the business lexicon and come up with terms that are all at once unctuous and pompous, impenetrable and threatening. Meeting this kind of vaporing is like meeting some smiling brute from a Coen Brothers' film: a psycho who seems to listen but never understands, who sits on the end of your bed and says he is *committed* to you and your family and your community and your country and to the whole world, but you wonder if he might soon go out and kill someone – or you, should you fall asleep.

We are committed to social responsibility. We are committed to doing the right thing. We want to make a positive difference in the world. This commitment began with our founder Ray Kroc. It continues today with our Board of Directors and executive leadership, is shared by our staff and franchisees, and reaches across our front counters to our customers and their communities.

This is McDonald's. It's McDonald's Corporate People Promise. McDonald's Corporate

People Promise comes with promises to animals as well. The Company has established 'the industry's first independent board of academic and animal protection experts. The Council has led to additional leadership initiatives for the well-being of cattle, poultry and hogs.' But we need not pick on McDonald's. Just about every company that takes on Corporate Social Responsibility expresses it in much the same way – in terms of *commitments* (and *enhancements*), as in:

We are committed to providing information to all our stakeholders in a clear and open way . . .

We are committed to establishing greater transparency and access to information . . .

At the State Revenue Office we are committed to providing you with a quality service and will make every effort to resolve the matter you have raised.

Commitment to these principles enhances the Department's ability to attract and retain staff, maximise staff potential and enhance the employment climate . . .

Sydney Water is always working to ensure you are supplied with clean, fresh water. To continue doing this, we occasionally need to shut off your water supply.

You might want to believe them. You might even persuade yourself that you do. But there's something about the way they talk that doesn't ring true. It doesn't

The cradle rocks above an abyss, and common sense tells us that our existence is but a brief crack of light between two eternities of darkness.

Vladimir Nabokov,
Speak, Memory

At the time of his retirement he offered the salient advice that he was worried 'politicians had lost touch with the bush', reflecting his ongoing commitment and concern for the interests of rural Victoria.

Condolence motion,
Victorian Parliament

ring false for that matter. In fact it doesn't ring at all. It's the verbal equivalent of a blank stare. The word *commitment* has something to do with it: why don't they say, we will do the right thing; we will provide information; we will establish . . . ? 'I am committed to the future of Africa': why don't I just look in the general direction of Nairobi and wave? It would mean as much. At the State Revenue Office, why don't they drop the advertising and get on with fixing it? But it also has something to do with taking us for mugs. It is one thing to tell people that the bun in the bag is a hamburger; that the company's mission was all but *benchmarked* by the Franciscans is something else entirely. What happened to 'the business of America is business'? Do they think we'll cook at home if they project themselves as anything less than selfless to a fault? Is it because in a world where you can persuade people there are forty-three beans in every cup, you come to believe that only a fool holds anything back? It seems more likely that language is the root of it: corporate language simply doesn't have the equipment to dissemble subtly.

We know how much they mean it when a letter of offer comes with the same laboured attempts at sweetening phrases as a letter of demand. It is all done to *serve you better*; or *enhance our services to better serve you*. A bank can't tell you that it is cutting a fee without setting this small gesture in the context of its *corporate social responsibility*, its *holistic approach* to munificence. And it can't tell you that in future it will bounce all cheques that overdraw your account by more than five cents, and hit you with a fee for doing it, without a pro forma that also tells you that it's *changing the way we honour payments which will overdraw accounts*, and they are telling us so we can *better manage the way you do your banking with us*.

There is no space in this sanctimonious clag for the light of the imagination. There is no room for a feeling properly felt. There is no room for an 'other' – which with writing is usually the reader. You cannot tell if the author of the words is genuine or not because they have no author. They are ritual words. It is as if, like someone with schizophrenia or depression, they are not quite of the real world. They have forgotten the language the rest of us speak.

If evidence is needed to support Francis Fukuyama's theory that we are at the end of history, the decline of public language might provide some. It will be 'a very sad time', Fukuyama wrote more than a decade ago. 'The struggle for recogniton, the willingness to risk one's life for a purely abstract cause, the irreducible ideological struggle that called for daring, courage, imagination and idealism, will be replaced by economic calculation, the endless solving of technical problems, environmental concerns, and the satisfaction of sophisticated human demands . . .' Perhaps not everyone will remember the Cold War so fondly; but it is easy to see a connection between his description of human concerns in the post-Cold War world and the language we now endure. The professional life may not yet be the *archetypal* life, but the line between the workplace and the rest of existence is certainly not as clear: words, ethics and ideals are all increasingly interchangeable and, thanks to radio, television and the internet, pervasive.

It may be that business, especially in its global manifestation, is unselfconsciously shaping a language of near perfect objectivity; a language stripped of ambiguity and variety, including the various interpretations that words are open to. You may be as clear as a cat with a furball, but better to speak in buzz words and clichés because there can be no argument with words that have no

---

I have a dream that one day this nation will rise up and live out the true meaning of its creed: 'We hold these truths to be self-evident: that all men are created equal.' I have a dream that one day on the red hills of Georgia the sons of former slaves and the sons of former slaveowners will be able to sit down together at a table of brotherhood. I have a dream that one day even the state of Mississippi, a desert state, sweltering with the heat of injustice and oppression, will be transformed into an oasis of freedom and justice. I have a dream that my four children will one day live in a nation where they will not be judged by the color of their skin but by the content of their character. I have a dream today.

Martin Luther King, *Address at the Lincoln Memorial*

meaning at their core. Eccentric and atypical behaviour among politicians – including loss of moral judgement – can often be explained by their inability to distinguish between the different codes that govern the world of business and the world of democratic government. Any politician who has to get through an interview can easily be caught up in the confusion inherent in 'building an online platform for integrated customer centric service delivery'; or 'adopting innovative methods for effectively chartering (sic) future paths for portal development and ultimately making customer interaction with government operations more effective' You can hear them saying it; and adding that these things are not done 'overnight', but within 'a reasonable time frame'.

The media is always the forcing ground. Listen to the coaches at the end of football matches and you will hear words straight from the corporate world, which is where their clubs now belong: 'we *zoned off*'; 'we stuck to the *game plan*'; 'we need more *flexibility* on the forward line': 'we were *committed* to the ball'. No player in the history of the game to c.1990 was *committed* to the ball. Now every player must be. We hear more of this corporate stuff – the team, the club, the four points – and less of the language of the self. What we are losing is language expressing character or imagination, which interests one human being in another, and from which the game's spirit springs. It is fading at the point we would expect to see it most plainly, the panting post-match interview. Sometimes in these brief cameos you can imagine you are witnessing the apotheosis of the postmodern, the human subject apparently dispensing with itself. And so it is sometimes with politicians.

Language tethers us to the world; without it we spin like atoms.

Penelope Lively,
Moon Tiger

ACHIEVE a user centric portal framework.

2nd Annual National Conference on Government Portals

The sublime is within the reach of public language – listen to Martin Luther King's speech on the steps of the Lincoln Memorial in 1963, then say it is not – but it is getting further from our grasp. This is partly because politics is played on a narrower field and one where inspiration and independent thought are not encouraged. The field is defined by ideological *think tanks* and players are professionals who work to a *game plan* or *strategy*. Words, being open to all kinds of interpretation including some that are not *on message*, are chosen only after strenuous *risk assessment*. If, like much else in contemporary politics, this sounds more like the corporate world than politics, get used to it. Political thought and speech has been entangling itself with the corporate stuff for years, and unless a way is found to separate them, in a generation or two few people will know that anything better once existed. We do not wait for Pericles, but we hope for something better from a politician than a poor imitation of a business consultant. When we read what follows we know we have an *issue* here, a *capability gap in terms of words*.

> I have flagged with the government my involvement to assist in resolving the issues that are impeding reconciliation. I would like to progress discussion with indigenous people to set in process the parameters of reconciliation.

Consciously or not, the Senator (or his staffer) was only attempting to speak the language of the locals. He was *value-adding* (or *adding alpha* as very refined managers say). *Value-adding* is a mantra of modern economics: it describes the increase in value that a particular manufacturing process, or design or labelling or some other *enhancement* brings to a product before its sale. Those who talk a lot about *value-adding* often sound as if they are trying to achieve the same effect with the language: they force it into a new mould, streamline it, give it *cachet*. They make it into a machine with a minimum of moving parts, but with constant *upgrades* and (naturally) *enhancements*. And if you want to get reconciliation taken seriously, you had better put your case in these terms. The Senator's imitation of the style is a remote sign of the gathering belief that the whole world – or such parts of it that function properly – can be understood either as a metaphor for free market economics and the management philosophies it has spawned, or as an actual consequence of them. That is to say, as an *outcome* or an *event*.

Many things that in the past simply happened, now happen as *events* or *episodes*. *Events* are to the natural world what *outcomes* are to the man-made – and like *outcomes* they must be managed. On the radio when the Weather Bureau says *weather* or *rain*, they are now inclined to add *event* to it. They will say, 'there has not been a *rain event* in the Mallee since February, but there have been a couple of *weather events* in the western district.' In the present climate Gene Kelly would sing 'Singin' in the Rain Event' and Billie Holiday 'Stormy Weather Event'. Nature does not easily give in to the new language: in a leaflet telling customers that their supply was about to be turned off, Sydney Water recently advised that 'times may vary depending upon the nature of the encounter problems associated with bad weather'. Rarely in history have sensible human beings found it so hard to say simple things.

Primo Levi was right: people who write and speak like this cannot be happy. It is said that a happy worker is a good worker, and what workers would not be happier if the sentences they write and read were less like a clogged drain? What if they were more like a babbling brook? If they were clear and yet contained an image or two and a bit of fun or verve; or had a sinew of imagination like this sentence taken at random from a page of William Faulkner: *Back running, tunnelled between the two sets of bobbing mule ears, the road vanishes beneath the wagon as though it were a ribbon and the front axle were a spool*? If that's too fanciful, what if we aimed to make it simple: as simple as, *Go wash them hands*, which appears on the same page of Faulkner. What's hard about that? There is no need to *implement* any-thing, or *strategise* about it, and no one ever says, *in terms of the bathroom,* or *in respect of the bathroom,* you should wash your hands in it. No one says, *Hopefully we can have your commitment to a scenario in terms of the ute which will have you in place in it within a reasonable timeframe, Rover*. We say, *Get in*, and Rover gets in. But the public language, which could easily stimulate our minds and have an effect like music on our souls, is drowning us in sludge.

Business idioms are one kind of flypaper for politicians: the media also lures them to its peculiar way with words. It has been said of the present leader of the Labor Party that he sounds like he's reading the news. That may depend on the ears of those who hear him, or the news they listen to; but it is certainly true that some politicians imitate their questioners so faithfully they sound like trainee TV news-hounds. The first Australian political leader to speak like this was 'Two Minute' Tim Fischer, the former Deputy Prime Minister. He was not the last. It would not surprise if one day they signed off their doorstops – 'Martin Ferguson, Parliament House, Canberra.'

'It's very clear, I think, from the totality of the Opposition's question and the totality of the Prime Minister's answer, exactly what the context of the answer was.'

Tony Abbott,
MHR

'I am not denying anything I didn't say.'
Brian Mulroney,
Canadian PM

INITIATE innovative strategies for portal measurement and review.

2nd Annual National
Conference on
Government Portals

You might say that there are worse things for a politician to sound like than a newsreader (a lame duck, for instance), but those who do the marketing, the gurus at party headquarters, will say it's a bummer – an unambiguous net negative. The political leader is meant to be in the story, not telling it. The newsreader is meant to tell the story, not be it. Any changes to this arrangement are bound to invite suspicion, and even contempt, especially in the almost certain event that real newsreaders are better at the job and better-looking. But if parrots mimic when threatened with rejection or death, why imagine struggling politicians will be immune? It's legitimacy they need, authority. Who better to imitate than a newsreader? Instinct drives them, not advice, which makes it hard to prevent and even harder to eradicate once the habit is formed.

Being adapted to its quarry – the profound, uncertain, elusive truth – language is often tentative. Much of the phrasing in truth-seeking language, including poetry, is provisional. Arguments and

stories are built on blocks or in layers, like an oil painting. The plots of novels, the truth of poems (like life) turn
on minute variations, nuance, an impulse, chance, a
shade of meaning. But in politics – and in marketing –
the pressure is away from the provisional and towards
the absolute. This is to say it's away from reality. *Yes* or
No are not the only honest answers in a complex, transi-
tional world. But in politics and business they are
demanded. The language that evolves is squeezed out of
this contradiction: the demand to be categorical, and the
necessity (and the instinct) to hedge. True, there are
plenty of downright lies and deliberate furphies. But
there are, as well, attempts to answer questions which,
politically speaking, are unanswerable.

Weasel words are no less the product of their environment than weasels are. In the diabolical environment
of politics, unreasoning forces throw up unreasoning
things like red herrings and dead cats, and fling them in
the path of journalists. Politicians come forth willing to
say anything, and without regard to ordinary civility.
Their opponents are rank hypocrites, they say: they've
heinous secret plans that all the outward signs disguise.
And often it emerges that these outrageous accusations
have some truth about them, because politics does
throw up hypocrites and liars. In keeping with the
evolution of such political animals, among journalists
horrible cynics emerge.

For the language the consequences are terrible: catch-
alls, clichés and nauseating platitudes are all rolled out.
Syntax is mangled. Reason goes up in smoke. The truth is
less significant than the political contest. The question
is not, *Which is the better argument?* It is *Who won?*

Or *What was the outcome*? Along with reason and enlightenment, the language goes out the window; and with the language go many opportunities for humour, spontaneity, originality and surprise.

Television news purports to tell us what is going on in the world. It tells us, however, in much the same way that the word *Biscuits* written on a biscuit jar, or *Gorilla* written on a gorilla cage, tells us about biscuits and gorillas. News on TV is not much more than *signage* – the current word for more than one sign; as in, 'God sent Moses a piece of *signage*' or, 'Moses had a *signage event* that *empowered* him *going forward*'. Naturally, the TV news cannot tell us everything, but it is the principal medium of information for the masses, the crucial medium of government and politics – and, of course, the sleekest of vehicles for marketing.

TV news is delivered from a certain elevation, and like it or not, must be taken seriously by everyone who relies on public opinion. Politicians, business people, football coaches and people with even bigger grievances, along with the

All was vague, contradictory, and unaccountable; and the Lord Deputy, advancing further and further into the green wilderness, began – like so many others before and after him – to catch the surrounding infection, to lose the solid sense of things, and to grow confused over what was fancy and what was fact.

Lytton Strachey,
Elizabeth and Essex

journalists, all bring to the daily news prefabricated grabs and all-purpose platitudes. If we are kind, we can forgive them on the Machiavellian basis that their work requires this of them, and the only sin is doing it badly. To give them a chance of going seamlessly into the world, government (and company) press releases have long been written in the language of the newspapers and electronic media. They offer a headline, an opening paragraph and a quote; and they hope that the media will run with it as if they wrote it themselves. So the language of the media and the language of politics are blended. If one is a peculiar, dishonest or debased language, the other is bound to become so.

In the media, sound-bites grow ever shorter and more tendentious, even if this also means they are misleading, inadequate or silly. TV news adopts a strange sentence structure to accompany images. It is, after all, a visual medium. When the technology for sound arrived, the old film directors did not take long deciding: where words and images compete, go with the image. It's the image they'll remember the next day, and the next week and possibly for the rest of their lives. Television reportage is weighted in the same way. The words over the image sound remote, staccato, disembodied. They serve as an almost subliminal support to the pictures. A school fire in January 2003 is reported: *Two hundred staff rallied together, some needing counselling, later inspecting the devastation first hand*. The sentence has been stitched together to match fleeting pictures of people in a meeting room; a person standing; a burnt building. And then the reporter eyeballs us and says: *It's been described as a phoenix rising from the ashes . . .* Thus another suburban drama has been turned into a soap.

'We shall fight on the beaches, we shall fight on the landing grounds, we shall fight in the fields and in the streets, we shall fight in the hills; we shall never surrender.'

Winston Churchill

In fact we have created a political process in which 'consensus' is the last thing the professionals want or need, a process that works precisely by turning the anger and fears and energy of the few — that handful of voters who can be driven by the fixed aspect of their own opinions — against the rest of the country.

Joan Didion, *New York Review of Books*

There is no solution to this: nothing at least that might be called *structural*. It's in the nature of the medium, and the medium is essentially one for marketing. After that, it's a medium for entertainment. Information and the public interest does not exactly come third, but rather has to fight for a place among the advertising and jokes. The principles of marketing are not the same as the principles of democracy. The first principle of marketing, according to some schools, is to 'turn needs into wants'. Whatever we take that to mean, it is probably not what most of us expect from our political system. But we are talking principles: talk realities and we begin to find common ground. Marketing asserts, first, the right to choice and, second, the right to manipulate you by any means short of extortion and blackmail into believing that there is no choice but to buy a particular product. This also is not what most of us would think desirable for politics. But while many of us would not see the ambitions of democracy and the ambitions of marketing as the same, we are sure to recognise similarities between such marketing ambitions and democratic practice. The language is bound to express this overlap.

Those old film-makers were right, of course. Pictures rule. To the extent that TV rules, pictures rule; and to the extent that TV is the most important medium of public life, the public language is at best a secondary consideration, and at worst indistinguishable from the language of marketing and entertainment. No wonder, then, that political parties become 'poll driven'; that their political strategies are essentially marketing strategies built on the same kinds of demographic research and replete with the same kinds of slogans and messages. No wonder that the trend in politics is increasingly towards sending messages, sometimes subliminally, to the increasingly narrow sections of the population that are reckoned to count politically. For the rest, governing the country seems to have been transformed (in Joan Didion's words) 'into a series of signals meant for someone else'.

The great screenwriter, Jean-Claude Carrière says, 'A film is complete when the screenplay is vanished'. So maybe the language suffers a slow death as the world becomes more like a film, or one at least which we understand as much through images as words. Is this what John Howard understood when he went to Bali after the bombs exploded? He was seen embracing the victims, grieving with them, and it must have been that people were comforted by these images because his approval ratings rose. Yet he spoke no notable words.

Likewise, although he was within easy helicopter range, President Bush announced victory in Iraq by arriving on the aircraft carrier *Abraham Lincoln* in a Viking jet. He wore full military attire, which was something President Eisenhower, an actual general, and President Kennedy, an actual war hero, never did. Nothing Bush said had a hope of matching the drama of the pictures. We can safely presume that nothing was intended to.

Pictures rule: but words define, explain, express, direct, hold together our thoughts and what we know. They lead us into new ideas and back to older ones. In the beginning was the Word. It might help everyone a little if among the *signage* in the newsroom – or the party room, or any room where decisions that concern the nation's life are made – there was one that quoted the writer Barry Lopez: 'Take care for the spiritual quality, the holy quality, the serious quality of the language.'

The competition policy reforms further improve the performance of government business enterprises through a program of regulation review, enhanced prices oversight, application of competitive neutrality principles and procedures for structural reform of public monopolies.

Australian Government

Language is a key issue of access for people from any non-English speaking culture. It affects the individual's ability to access and use services and knowledge of services.

Human Rights Commission

My advice to any young Australian writer
whose talents have been recognised would be to
do steerage, stow away, swim, and seek London,
Yankeeland, or Timbuctoo – rather than stay in
Australia till his genius turn to gall, or beer.
Or, failing this – and still in the interests of
human nature and literature – to study
elementary anatomy, especially as it applies to
the cranium, and then shoot himself carefully
with the aid of a looking glass.

Henry Lawson

A PERSON COULD BE lynched for saying it, but among the few sad truths of Australia's existence is the fact that our public language is not heir to much native poetry or song, not in a direct line at least. Few truly rousing words have been left on the public record. Perhaps the deeds were not sufficient to inspire them. No great cause inspired European settlement here. Self-government came without the necessity to fight for it. Federation was at most an elegant compromise. To the extent that the new nation's laws and institutions derived from and deferred to Britain so would the language of its foundation. 'Empirespeak', Chris Wallace-Crabbe called it:

The stuff was rich as mother's milk.
I couldn't see it didn't fit,
making it do so anyway,
eliding what was grossly wrong.

In London, around the time the First Fleet was anchoring in Port Jackson, they were uttering words of distinction; words marrying intellect with moral passion. About slavery for instance: 'Thus sir, has the perversion of British commerce carried misery instead of happiness to one whole quarter of the globe,' William Pitt told the Commons.

False to the very principles of trade, misguided in our policy, and unmindful of our duty, what astonishing – I had almost said, what irreparable – mischief we have brought upon that continent. How shall we ever repair this mischief? How shall we hope to obtain, if it be possible, forgiveness from heaven for those enormous evils we have committed, if we refuse to make use of those means which the mercy of Providence hath still reserved to us for wiping away the guilt and shame with which we are now covered?

'Covered' in guilt and shame. 'Wiping' it away. We can only wonder at these sentiments.

When the British reached Australia's shores they seemed to lose their inspiration. The first public occasion at Sydney Cove, on the day the convicts were landed, began with the Judge Advocate describing the legal basis of the Governor's untrammelled power. When he had finished the marines fired off a volley and played the first bars of 'God Save the King', whereupon the Governor delivered a speech to the convicts that appears to have been mainly a sort of church camp harangue. Good behaviour would be rewarded, he said; and bad

'What, Sir, you damn'd scoundrel, never was a man troubled with such a lot of blackguards as I am. Take care, Sir, I am looking out for you.'

William Bligh

'It cannot in the opinion of His Majesty's Government be classified as slavery in the extreme acceptance of the word without the risk of some terminological inexactitude.'

Winston Churchill

behaviour would be severely punished. It was a penal colony, so at the foundation of the British Empire in Australia, the Governor considered it his most pressing duty to tell the men that if they were seen in the women's quarters they would be fired at with ball.

While British Governors in New South Wales were laying about their charges with moral platitudes, the Americans were inspiring each other with arguments about the rights of man. The period of Australia's foundation gave the Americans Tom Paine, Thomas Jefferson, James Madison and George Washington, who was not the most gifted orator but his retirement speech, written for him by Alexander Hamilton, was more memorable than any speech made by our first half-dozen Governors. In fact the first half-dozen Governors failed to say a single thing that anyone remembers.

We have never been strong on language: good at inventing words, dab hands with similes, deft at laconic understatement, but our words have never come rolling like they do from Americans. Perhaps we needed a Mississippi or a Missouri or a Civil War or slavery to inspire us.

With few exceptions our leaders were not loquacious. Menzies had a claim to eloquence but even his supporters were inclined to say that if he had one fault it was inveterate speechifying. Something of the style can be seen in a film made around 1932 outside the then spanking new Parliament House in Canberra. The Hon. Joseph Aloysius Lyons PM steps forward to the camera and, brushing away the flies, introduces himself. He then shoos away some more flies and introduces his deputy. One by one the members of the Cabinet come forward mechanically brushing, and utter their names in either quite astonishing nasal twangs or, in a few cases, English private school accents. The scene at once reflects the deep democratic character of Australia and its stubborn refusal to be articulate. The Lyons film was made at about the time Franklin Delano Roosevelt became President of the United States. At his inauguration in 1933 Roosevelt delivered a great speech about the Depression and its implications for the American people and American capitalism. It is quite impossible to imagine FDR before a camera outside the White House without something to say, or some performance to put on.

In their different ways the two godparents of our existence, the United States and Great Britain, have had it all over us with language: the US with their sheer self-confidence, which made them free, inventive, and apparently driven by an internal rhythm, like Don Bradman batting; and the English, who it seemed to us spoke the language as it was meant to be spoken – a notion which certainly encouraged imitation in genteel Australians, and perhaps

To win speech is to be sovereign, at least within a little time and space. It means filling the air and your neighbour's ears, making some kind of union between your own breath, the whimsy of your lips and the souls of those who hear you.

Alan Atkinson, *The Commonwealth of Speech*

In olden days a
  glimpse of
  stocking
Was looked on as
  something
  shocking.
Now, heaven knows,
Anything goes!

Cole Porter

an even more concerted slovenliness in the vulgar ones. But it was not in our breeding to be eloquent. Perhaps there was too much inner chaos; caught as we were between wanting to be like both the civilised English and the self-assured Americans. Those Americans were born eloquent and were still crooning eloquently on our TVs and radios when we were kids. We whistled 'When It's Springtime in the Rockies' while we worked, and 'Old Man River', 'The Banana Boat Song' and 'Oklahoma' – we could sing just about the whole soundtrack of *Oklahoma*. Put the words in our mouths and we'd sing them, but they didn't come out the way they did for other people. Generally we could make ourselves understood but not in the way other people, including those New Australians, seemed to. We put it down to modesty or the sensible conservation of breath. We did not enjoy the sound of our own voices like they did, or getting high-flown or sentimental at the drop of a hat.

At the birth of the nation, Henry Lawson spoke to the ordinary people in a voice that at its best stands comparison with Mark Twain's. Lawson's rhythmic, unadorned prose did not find its way into the public language however. It was, perhaps, too elegantly earthbound. By contrast, whether he was telling listeners that 'his whole being trembles with an unuttered prayer', or urging the colonies to adopt a uniform rail gauge, the Father of Federation, Sir Henry Parkes, often seemed to be attempting to take off.

And what prayer made Henry Parkes's being tremble? It was, as he told them in his famous 1881 Tenterfield oration, that 'the whole of the British possessions may remain forever forming parts of one beneficent Empire such as the world has never seen'. When Australians had done in peace what the Americans had done by war, and done it 'without breaking the ties that hold them to the mother country'; when 'the name of an Australian [was] equal to that of a Briton'; when they were 'masters of the South Seas'; when their Governor General 'would be able to hold a court . . . as attractive as that of the monarchs of the Old World' – then, Australians would no longer 'dream of going home'.

If Parkes's rhetoric did not take wing it was partly because of the argument he was advancing: the prayer that made him tremble was for a compromise, a bit of this and a bit of that; as if it were possible to achieve what the Americans had without separating from the mother country. Such ideas as his speech-making proposed were born stale or half-baked; such emotions as it stirred always included the emotion of relief – the comforter that we could have our cake and eat it, that we could leave without going away.

A powerful agent is the right word. Whenever we come upon one of those intensely right words in a book or a newspaper the resulting effect is physical as well as spiritual, and electrically prompt.
Mark Twain

When you are using metaphor, do not mix it up. That is, don't start by calling something a swordfish and end by calling it an hourglass.
Strunk and White,
The Elements of Style

Rhetoric may need something less ambivalent; an unalloyed sentiment or ideal like liberty or justice, or freedom from hunger or fear. It was precisely these sorts of abstractions that Australian statesmen shied from. Alfred Deakin was loath to put 'any metaphysical argument upon the rights of man'. Rather, it was the unequalled material equality existing in Australia and not any abstract principle that made the case for equal political rights. The case was, as it were, the self-evident truth of colonial evolution; an empirical fact, something to be observed and explained by rational minds. Demagogic and utopian elements of the labour movement might make more rousing claims, but the same evolutionary principle applied. William Lane explained the Australian dream as 'one of those periodic tides which change and alter the whole life of the human race; it is the first pulsation of another of that series of upheavals which through countless cycles of evolution's phases have uplifted the senseless cell of protoplasmic life to the exalted station whereon the white man stands'.

Like his utopian experiment in Paraguay, Lane's rhetoric bogged down. The Americans of the time were no less eloquent about human rights because they were lynching human beings. But Lane's racial theories were primary and they sunk his ideal in the swamp of social Darwinism, while the American one, strung on Jeffersonian and other eloquent balloons, floated above the ugly reality. It was not confined to the radical Lane: upon the federation of the colonies into a Commonwealth under the Crown, the liberal Deakin said that keeping the place white was the one thing upon which a consensus always existed. Until then it was much as the liberal lawyer George Higinbotham had remarked twenty-five years earlier, 'impossible to find half a dozen politicians united for promoting . . . the national interest upon some principle in which they are all agreed'.

The founding moments in Australian history threw up no founding ideals: none at least that were articulated. Even the Labor Party was for *socialism sans doctrines*, as a French visitor put it. There were the ideals of British civilisation, British institutions, the British Empire and the British race. There was also the ideal of compromise; the compromise that would, to paraphrase a wit of those times, found a new nation under the glorious Southern Cross and make sugar and meat cheaper; the compromise of capital and labour reconciled in minimum wages and arbitrated disputes. Australia was born in compromise and with a pronounced leaning to the practical and the laconic. These are very sound – even Socratic – values and they have worked as well here as they have in the United States where, along with outrageous confidence, they are also held to be an essential part of the national character.

Robust and useful as these qualities are, they do not provide the foundations of a rhetorical tradition. Laconic and inventive, yes; but short on depth, ideas and musicality. Today's non-language is everywhere in the economically developed world, but it does seem more pervasive here. British politicians, Tony Blair among them, are infinitely more fluent, as are their journalists and commentators. The President of the United States is not impressive, but sometimes those around him are. After what we are accustomed to, an interview with the American heavyweight conservative, Richard Armitage, is almost thrilling for the whole sentences he conjures, the deft and subtle phrasing, the combined grace and menace, the rare sight of a public figure effortlessly thinking his way into perfectly arranged words. We watch him and think that so long as they have such powers of speech our relationship with the US could never be equal, even if our GDPs and armies were.

Teamwork is critical to effective continuous improvement and standardization. Individuals can support the team by taking responsibility for the success of the team following through on commitments, contributing to discussions, actively listening to others, getting your message across clearly, giving useful feedback, accepting feedback easily.

Management instruction

Here we make do with language, as we make do with low rainfall and thin soil and bits of wire. Our politicians have long been in the habit of making phrases as if they were door sausages to keep out draughts, and tossing us clichés like bones to dogs – or, as one Premier used to say, like wheat to chooks. Our casual pragmatism attracts us to clichés and makes us reluctant to discard them. What is a cliché after all, but something like an old wheelbarrow or darned sock we can use over and over again; something with which we 'make do'. Our natural liking for them might be one reason why we were such suckers for the technocratic clichés of the eighties. It might be why people we might have expected to know better, in schools and universities and other places that deal with human intelligence and emotions, and banks and other businesses that deal with people face-to-face and ought to communicate plainly and persuasively, also took up this non-language – and even made it a *core value*. And, indeed, why the population at large takes it lying down: it is how we have always taken it.

Australia's native language bloomed in late-nineteenth-century popular literature, but it was not recast and regenerated in Australia as it was in America by film and music. Cole Porter, Hoagy Carmichael and George Gershwin seemed to take as much pleasure in their mastery of language as they did in the genius of their music. Australians, like the rest of the world, took pleasure in it too. To that extent the tin-pan alley lyrics belonged to the world, but they came from American life and were as purely American as the choreography of the

O'Shenendoah, I
long to see you
Away, you rolling
river!

Shenendoah

This requires a
commitment to
the provision of
adequate data so that
informed evaluation
can occur. There
must be a
commitment to
the provision of
statistical information
that will facilitiate
effective monitoring
and evaluation
strategies and a
commitment to the
implementation of
changes that are
identified as
necessary following
evaluation.

Human Rights and Equal
Opportunity Commission,
speech

frontier in a Hollywood western, or of a street in an American *noir* film. When Fred Astaire and Judy Garland sang 'Walk Down the Avenue' it could be no avenue but a New York avenue, and when Billie Holiday sang 'The Man I Love', the man who would one day come along could only be American.

This kind of poetry we never had, and it is of no importance to the argument that few countries did. The argument is simply that we have sung very few songs of our own. In the whole history of Australia there are surely not half a dozen known to more than ten per cent of the population: 'Waltzing Matilda' (a Scots tune), 'Click Go the Shears', perhaps 'The Banks of the Condamine'. The great majority of the songs we sang before the Americans were Scots, Irish and English and none of them – with the greatest respect – has the power of 'Shenendoah'.

Our national anthem of course we borrowed from Britain for most of the first eighty years of our nationhood, and then took up a dirge of local origin. The lyrics to only a few national anthems rise to inspiring heights, but it is just as true that few surpass 'Advance Australia Fair' for passivity, monotony and banality. No ideal is asserted and none defended. There is no attack at all. Put aside 'The Marseillaise' and the 'Star-Spangled Banner' with which nothing else compares; even the New Zealand anthem leaves Australia's for dead. New Zealand's is thick with ideas and ideals, including God, peace and hospitality, and full of resolute determination to defend them. 'Advance Australia Fair' is simply thick, and even more woefully at odds with the vernacular than 'God Save the Queen'.

Before patriots declare this line of reasoning un-Australian, remember that it is plainly no one's fault, and no bad thing sometimes, to lack both the capacity and the willingness to sell oneself in carefully scripted verbal flourishes. So long as we're required to sing 'our home is girt by sea' we are not likely to start putting our hands over our hearts. And who else in the world wants a leader who sounds like George W. Bush? The US was born loquacious and had this facility invigorated by the neo-classical fashion of which Lincoln was the most influential example, and the Civil War from which his words were forged. Who wants eloquence if it takes a Civil War to get it?

But the US was also born holding certain things to be self-evident. It was born with a philosophy – republican, democratic and from time to time fiercely Christian. It had a Constitution worth quoting and a Declaration of Independence. It is the place where the most egregious abuses of language occur and are disseminated, but for their own purposes they have a great tradition on which

Australians all
   let us rejoice
For we are young
   and free
We've golden soil
   and wealth for toil
Our home is girt
   by sea
   Advance Australia Fair

Oh, say can you
   see, by the dawn's
   early light,
What so proudly
   we hail'd at the
   twilight's last
   gleaming?
   The Star-Spangled Banner

Arise, children
   of the fatherland,
The day of glory
   has arrived,
Against us tyranny's
Bloody standard
   is raised.
      La Marseillaise

to build and fall back. Here, for want of any rousing local themes, the most articulate leaders have either, like Menzies, fallen back upon the British, or like Whitlam, upon antiquity – and both upon the law. There is no cache of diamond-like ideas, no deathless phrases from immortal statesmen. Put out your speechwriter's shingle in Australia and you will be asked mainly for jokes; and after jokes sporting analogies, and also to tidy up the prose. There is mateship and Anzac and to these, and one or two other canards of our singularity or virtue, they repeatedly return.

The state lies in all languages of good and evil;
and whatever it says, it lies – and whatever it
has, it has stolen . . . Confusion of the language
of good and evil; I offer you this sign as the
sign of the state.

Friedrich Nietzsche, *Thus Spake Zarathustra*

'We need to counter the shock wave of the evil-
doer by having individual rate cuts accelerated
and by thinking about tax rebates.'

George W. Bush

IN THE AFTERMATH OF Al-Qaeda's attack on New York and
Washington, Philip Roth told *Le Figaro*: 'Language is
always a lie, above all public language.' He seemed to be
saying that as the volume of public language had been
greater since 9/11, so had the volume of lies. He might also
have observed that never has the language so lacked the
capacity to utter truth. Those who spoke and wrote the
public language in the past commonly have lacked motivation to say honestly what they meant or to speak in
enlivening ways, but now they lack the words as well.
When George W. Bush speaks, all Philip Roth hears, he
says, are the voices of ventriloquists.

Philip Roth is not the only one to imagine a ventrilo-
quist's hand up George W. Bush's jumper. We all pretty
well take it for granted that our leaders are either scripted,
or in other ways programmed by their advisers. Only some
of us mind, and even then we're often inclined to think the
ventriloquists might make more sense than the people we

elected. And the ventriloquists make them say things we want to hear. Say *jobs*, they tell them before they go out to meet the media: say *growth*, say *evil*, say *liberal*, say *women*, say *strong*, say *humble* – say *strong but humble*. And they say them. And becuse they have been market-researched, they comfort us as familiar things comfort us, as clichés comfort us. Strong but humble: sounds good to me, we say. Can't get enough of it, we say. Amen.

To be *strong but humble* is a mantra of modern business leadership. The idea did not begin with managerialism, of course, but it is possible that the US President or one of his advisers picked it up in business school. No American administration has ever contained so many CEOs. In the Presidential debates during the last US election campaign, George W. Bush recommended being strong; but he also said, 'Ours will be a humble nation.' Against any estimate of truth this hardly rates above, 'I will never, ever introduce a GST.' It is as untrue and almost certainly as calculated, and we may confidently assume that it was no more sincere. And it is why speakers of the public language should be pursued relentlessly, not only for the facts they aver and the thoughts they profess, but for the words they use.

Our leaders in Washington are forever invoking him and in Australia we have nothing comparable, so let's go back to Lincoln and his Gettysburg Address. Or to Pericles' address to the Athenians during the Peloponnesian Wars. Here are two famous examples of public language. More than two thousand years apart, both memorialise those who died in battle, both seek meaning in their deaths. They can still persuade us that every word is true. Here is Pericles (or at least what Thucydides recalled of it):

> ... what their eyes showed plainly must be done they trusted their own valour to accomplish, thinking it more glorious to defend themselves and die in the attempt than to yield and live. From the reproach of cowardice, indeed, they fled, but presented their bodies to the shock of battle; when insensible of fear, but triumphing in hope, in the doubtful charge they instantly dropped – and thus discharged the duty which brave men own owed their country.

We can tell that Pericles did not show his speech to any firm of political or business consultants, or a team of ministerial advisers, because he has described the soldiers' deaths without saying they were *committed* or *showed commitment*. There is no *hopefully* in it. They did not seek, according to Pericles at least, any *enhancement* of

---

Good morning and welcome. It is a pleasure to be here this morning to share the initiatives and strategies that the Department of X is implementing to better manage diversity in our workplace. The Department of X understands and values the importance of continually improving workplace culture and firmly supports the principles of organisational diversity and equal opportunity. Commitment to these principles enhances the Department's ability to attract and retain staff, maximise staff potential and enhance the employment climate, which ultimately will improve the services we deliver to our diverse client base.

Victorian Government

their reputations. They saw duty as owed their country, not *in terms of* it. The sentences are full of verbs, empty of cliché and airy euphemisms. The dead are not the *fallen*. Death is death and not an *outcome*. There is no *closure*. In our world you might think that life is not worth living without *closure*.

And here is Lincoln, also verb-filled, in what William Safire called 'the best short speech since the Sermon on the Mount', at Gettysburg after the battle in 1863:

> Four score and seven years ago our fathers brought forth on this continent, a new nation, conceived in liberty, and dedicated to the proposition that all men are created equal. Now we are engaged in a great civil war, testing whether that nation, or any nation so conceived and so dedicated, can long endure. We are met on a great battlefield of that war. We have come to dedicate a portion of that field, as a final resting place for those who here gave their lives that that nation might live. It is altogether fitting and proper that we should do this. But in a larger sense, we cannot dedicate – we cannot consecrate – we cannot hallow – this ground. The brave men, living and dead, who struggled here, have consecrated it far above our poor power to add or detract. The world will little note, nor long remember, what we say here, but it can never forget what they did here . . .

Not so: as it turned out the speech outlived the deed. But one brave verb keeps the deed alive. 'Struggled'. He might have chosen from a dozen clichés or dressed it up with an adverb (*heroically*, *manfully*, *gallantly*). Instead, like Pericles' soldiers presenting 'their bodies to the shock of battle', Lincoln chose a word that reaches into the imagination and flicks a little switch that illuminates the truth for us. 'What they did here' is contained in that word, 'struggled'. Read aloud, it can make you shudder. This is what is meant by the power of words.

There is another famous example of public language, also commemorating the fallen, hardly less powerful and also a wonder of rhetoric; the speech Shakespeare gave Mark Antony at Julius Caesar's funeral.

Friends, Romans, countrymen, lend me your ears:
I come to bury Caesar, not to praise him.
The evil that men do lives after them,
The good is oft interred with their bones.

In defining our values, we have formed a range of acceptable and non-acceptable behaviours, which contribute to the success of implementation. Behaviours which indicate that we are complying with values and contra which indicate that we are not. For example, a key contra behaviour, that we are currently focusing on that was identified through our values, is employees displaying disrespectful behaviour towards clients and/or other staff members. The department is committed to providing a positive working environment free from intimidation, ridicule and harassment: disrespect or behaviour of this nature does not match this commitment nor does it match our organizational values, therefore, it will not be tolerated. In the varied and often challenging work environments that our employees face, it is important that we are continually improving how we manage such behaviour and that we have an effective strategy . . . (etc).

Victorian Government

But Antony's speech, while much like the other two, is also very different. Among other things it is an early example of political spin: he puts a spin on Caesar's death, or rather a counter-spin to the assassins' actions and especially to Brutus: 'For Brutus is an honourable man' and 'I am no orator, as Brutus is':

But were I Brutus,
And Brutus Antony, there were an Antony
Would ruffle up your spirits and put a tongue
In every wound of Caesar, that should move
The stones of Rome to rise and mutiny.

In Antony's speech we have a Roman (or Elizabethan) prototype for *dog whistling* – the name now given to the trick of tapping the political potential of suppressed prejudice, fear and envy through apparently harmless but carefully 'coded' words, and turning it against the rest of the country. Antony knows 'the power of speech to stir men's blood', and his speech, to use his own word, is intended to do 'mischief'. His words ring true, but conceal the truth of his real purpose.

We are used to this. The constant fog of lies and half-lies, filtered truth, information, misinformation, disinformation – spin and counter-spin – is endemic to the information age. But this age did not invent it. The Greeks wrote voluminously on the subject of rhetoric and its potential for both good and evil works. 'I will give him soft talk', Medea says before she lays the direst of all traps for Jason. We've been trying to tell the difference between soft talk and hard truth ever since. George Orwell recognised the signs half a century ago. In 1939, the French film-maker Jean Renoir saw himself living at a time when 'everyone lies; governments, radios, movies, newspapers'. He was right beyond doubt, and he was far from the only one to notice. The lies are just as pervasive and oppressive now, and take ever more ingenious forms.

Joined to a brilliant understanding of their hearts and minds, Antony's words bring the mob to mistake his ambition for a noble cause. Indeed he *ennobles* them – though today we would make do with *empowers*. Whatever it is he does to them, he also serves himself in doing it. And every time we hear a politician speak, a fight breaks out between our need to believe and our instinct to distrust. The struggle is because the power of words, as the Czech playwright and former president, Vaclav Havel, said a decade ago, 'is neither immediate nor clear-cut . . . Words that electrify society with their freedom and truthfulness are matched by words that mesmerise, deceive, inflame, madden . . . The selfsame word can at one time be the cornerstone of peace, while

Examine your words well, and you will find that even when you have no motive to be false, it is a very hard thing to say the exact truth, even about your own immediate feelings – much harder than to say something fine about them which is *not* the exact truth.

George Eliot, *Adam Bede*

It is to be noted that the methodology would become clearer and clearer as each step is put into practice enhancing the understanding of the scenario and help in fine-tuning the procedure to suit particular situations . . .

Knowledge Management, Information Needs of Clients

at another, machine-gun fire resounds in its every syllable.'

By way of example we might compare the US President's address to the Congress after September 11 with a speech made by Boris Yeltsin after the attempted coup in Moscow in 1991. The Bush speech had some resoundingly good lines, but it was also debilitated by cliché and a tone of Hollywood vengeance. It was, moreover, as Philip Roth complained, too plainly stitched together by other hands. No doubt it moved many Americans. But a fragment of Yeltsin's little speech has a more universal power. Addressing directly the parents of three young men who died defending their new freedom, he said: 'Forgive me, your President, that I could not defend, could not save your sons.' Words can bestow nobility on both those who speak them and those about whom they are spoken. They can do this even if they are not literally true, or the speaker is not widely regarded as a noble person. They can make us surrender, of themselves.

It may be mischief, but Antony's is stirring, memorable mischief: mischief made by someone who respects and knows the powers of language. For the most part our own leaders are less eloquent: less than Shakespeare naturally enough, and less than Havel; but also less eloquent than not so long ago leaders had to be. Eloquence is no guarantee of truth. Antony's speech is one proof of that. There are countless others. During and long after the First World War the public language was invaded by grotesque euphemisms for outrageous death and mutilation. Generally they were planted in perfectly constructed sentences. Some of them, long since turned to fossils, can still be heard on Anzac Day. Anything rather

We need words to keep us human. Being human is an accomplishment like playing an instrument. It takes practice.

Michael Ignatieff,
The Needs of Strangers

The information needs identifier (INI) would discover, as a bye-product (sic), several ideas, tools, methods and techniques of satisfying clients in meeting their needs as well as design new and novel information services and products to meet those needs.

Knowledge Management,
Information Needs of
Clients

than speak of death and the chance of meaninglessness. But eloquence gives truth a chance. For Aristotle rhetoric was a dangerous weapon, but one that truth must take up or be defeated.

Now, through the media, our leaders have learned, or at least their advisers have, that they still have the power 'to stir men's blood', but by less articulate means: with mantras, a well-placed platitude on the radio, a bit of cant tossed lightly to a press pack, a gesture on TV. All these will do as well as any speech to conceal the truth or hold the populace in thrall. Perhaps after the twin towers and the Bali bombing, nothing adequate could be said. Perhaps that old line about words being inadequate at times like this is more than a banality. However, it is more likely that the absence of memorable words to make some sense of the tragedy was a sign that politicians reckon words are inferior to images, especially images of grieving with the families of the victims. It's a symptom of language's declining status, and you can see the same symptoms at pretty well any funeral – or wedding, or board meeting.

Political terminology is never adequate to the multitudinous reality it seeks to define. Likewise, political leaders, staring down forests of microphones and lenses while journalists quiz them about that reality, invariably lack the inhuman skill to give answers that are both definitive and truthful. They develop other skills instead. They learn to say 'We are committed to this, yes, at this point in time, absolutely, Michelle'. Politics is a wrestling match with chaos (or smoke), and it prizes those who seem best able to impose their will upon the impossible. Successful politicians are those who can come up with a picture of things that approximates the view from where the rest of us are standing. Good ones do this by changing our view to theirs. The hacks seek out our view and try to make it their own. In Australia, for more than a decade, a government made the reality economic. Anyone who stepped outside was declared exiled, feral or wet. This was the political reality of the phrase *the main game*. No game is quite so 'main' today. The government keeps redefining the reality: one minute it is *battlers*, then the economy, then the bush, then immigration, personal security, national security, war. The political expression is *setting the agenda*. Every time a government succeeds in *setting the agenda*, or re-setting it, they re-set the language.

The Labor government, particularly its Treasurer, Paul Keating, introduced dozens of new words and phrases to the public language, and almost all of them at least putatively described an economic reality. To be part of the political culture, to be able to have a say, you had to master this language. Bob Hawke, the Prime Minister in those revolutionary times, was famed as an advocate, but sometimes it seemed that words were less the medium of his expression than just so many bloody obstacles placed in the way of making people see what he bloody saw. When speaking off the cuff he embarked on his sentences like a madman with a club in a dark room: he bumped and crashed around for so long his listeners became less interested in what he was saying than the prospect of his escape. When at last he emerged triumphantly into the light we cheered, not for the gift of enlightenment, but as we cheer a man who walks away from an avalanche or mining accident. And he raised his tremendous eyebrow as if to say, 'Now you see, for I have told you'. For a decade R. J. Hawke murdered speech, and politically it cost him nothing.

John Kerin, the man Hawke chose to replace Paul Keating as Treasurer, suffered a different fate. To the language in general Kerin did no harm, but one day at a press conference it became clear that he did not know the language that mattered. He did not know or could not remember what GOS

The English-speaking world may be divided into (1) those who neither know nor care what a split infinitive is; (2) those who do not know, but care very much; (3) those who know and condemn; (4) those who know and distinguish. Those who neither know nor care are the vast majority, and are a happy folk, to be envied by most of the minority classes.

H.W. Fowler, *Modern English Usage*

stood for. A journalist reminded him that it stands for *Gross Operating Share*. It was a phrase from *the main game*. Hawke sacked Kerin the next day. That was 1991.

By 1996 regionalism was the agenda: you had to learn *empowerment* and re-learn *community*, and *the bush* and all its alleged genuine, down-to-earth, common-sense, never-give-in, true-blue mateship sorts of Australian qualities. (*The bush* itself is a catchword specific to these times. In much of rural Australia for most of last century it was known as *the country*, and people who lived in the cities also knew it by that name.) In more recent times, *the bush* has had to give way to national security; and again new words were found to direct us to the new imperatives of life. Some of the blandest were the most misleading. *We don't want those sort of people here* (the sort that would throw their children into the sea) was sublimely suburban. But *we will decide who comes here and the circumstances in which they come* is a proposition with which no one could disagree. After the 2001 election no one could doubt the power of words or their capacity to carry messages way beyond their literal meanings.

There have been other shifts in modern times. This year on Anzac Day, when the national anthem had been sung at the 'now traditional' Collingwood–Essendon football match at the MCG, an ABC commentator was moved to say that all Australians hearing what he'd just heard would give thanks to those men who had defended 'the Australian lifestyle'. Everyone seemed to agree that this characterisation of Anzac was fair enough in the circumstances.

All successful politicians must be at least competent in the first part of Aristotelian dialectics, which is to rebut

The words of his mouth were smoother than butter, but war was in his heart: his words were softer than oil, yet were they drawn swords.

Psalm 55

And although there is no substitute for merit in writing, clarity comes closest to being one. Even to a writer who is being intentionally obscure or wild of tongue we can say, 'Be obscure clearly! Be wild of tongue in a way we can understand!' Even to writers of market letters, telling us (but not telling us) which securities are promising, we can say, 'Be cagey plainly! Be elliptical in a straightforward fashion!'

Strunk and White,
The Elements of Style

their opponents' case and persuasively put their own. But success depends on persuading the judge; or at least it did until the skills of modern marketing and research made it possible to second-guess the judge – which is to say, the people – instead. Inevitably the rhetorical skills grow weaker as the market research grows stronger. The issue is not decided in the parliament, but in the polling – and on the television. It's decided very largely by how often we judges hear the words we want to hear. When we hear them, and confirm them, not with our vote, but our voting *intention*, the words become sacrosanct. They become the narrative, the *story*. The *story* says this is how we got here (by economic reform, or by sacrifice, or by the *values* of the *bush*, or *community*, or by willingness to undertake adventures), so this is what matters. Those who do not know or respect the story must live outside the tribe. It is not Nazi Germany, but it doesn't always feel like democracy when the only reality seems to be that of the ruling group.

The difference between a dictatorship and a poll-driven democracy is that dictators kill or incarcerate their own citizens for political reasons. Dictatorships will not stand doubt: propaganda is used to create certainty, with terror in reserve. Democracies don't do this. But the language of modern politics is increasingly ruthless about doubters, or even people with imagination. Parties stay *on strategy*, leaders *on message*, and the *message* and the *strategy* are both drawn from the polls; which means that anyone who thinks differently may be interpreted as resisting the will of the people. The language is constructed so that it never leads the mind to those places minds naturally go: towards mysteries, contradictions, multitudes.

Modern political language has this much in common with propaganda. And something in common with war, which is also conducted according to strategies. As with defence forces (or bureaucracies – wherever careers are carved out) political practitioners are prone to believe their own bullshit. Words and phrases that began life as convenient catch-alls for skating over complex problems become indisputable truth, the last word in human understanding. Almost talismanic powers are ascribed to ridiculous words like *aspirational*. *Aspirational* voters, we are told, are people who want a better life for themselves and their families. And we wonder if we have ever met someone who wanted a worse life. *Aspirationals* are distinguished by their desire to get on in life. And we wonder if the same was not true of our own generation, and our parents and grandparents and pretty well everyone who ever made a life here. The difference is, we can only suppose, that it took until 2002 to find just the right word. A verb version is no doubt hatching somewhere in the dark.

The cliché organises life; it expropriates people's identity; it becomes ruler, defence lawyer, judge and the law.
Vaclav Havel,
Disturbing the Peace

To the man in the
  street who, I'm
  sorry to say
Is a keen observer
  of life;
The word
  'intellectual'
  suggests right
  away
A man who's
  untrue to his wife
W.H. Auden, 'Shorts'

The limits of my language mean the limits of my world.
Ludwig Wittgenstein, *Tractatus Logico-Philosophicus*

In the mid-nineties the word *battlers* seemed to work with the Liberal Party focus groups, so wherever the pollies went it went with them. Finding their focus groups liked *battlers* too, the other side decided they belonged to everyone and started trotting out *battlers* wherever they went, including places it would not willingly go: in caravan parks, Kim Beazley said, there were 'some of the most *battling* Australians'. By then everyone who was not a *battler* was at risk of being called an *elite*, even if they didn't have a non-business-related 4-wheel drive. Drinking *café latte* was enough. In the rush to win the *battlers'* hearts, everyone appeared to forget that fifteen years earlier not a few battlers might have qualified as *bludgers*; and for much of human history, including much of ours, what are now called *aspirationals* were called philistines and social climbers. The 1920s, for instance, was an era of *aspirationals* and look what happened. And you have to wonder if the decline of language and the decline of history is not a material aid to the progress of idiocy.

Political and corporate thinking have merged in this development. On both sides the fashion is for *strategies* and *outcomes*. The latter is a modern portmanteau to hold such words as *result, consequence, upshot, product, effect, return* and *happenstance*, which are all subtly different and don't suggest as *outcome* does that everything in the world is, or can be, governed by *strategies*. Without *outcomes* you can't have *accountability*, another portmanteau to replace more challenging concepts like *integrity, honesty, decency, truth* and *justice*, and to give people with the capacity to do good a reason to do nothing. So long as it runs on the principle of *accountability*, a business or department is less likely to profess, practise or even know anything about *imagination, courage, initiative, reflection* or *generosity* (to name just a few), which have been priceless human qualities until now and great aids to getting at the truth. It is even possible that the fashion for *accountability* encourages the use of dead words – because what is dead contains no threat.

The sibling of *accountability* is *transparency*, which in the new language is intended to denote that the public are able to see what's going on. You will see it in the financial pages; it crops up regularly in the parliament. Companies and government departments frequently include it in their mission statements. In most cases they are *committed* to it. *Transparency* is desirable, but when you see the word so often, you can't help wondering if it's not hiding something. There must be other words to describe what amounts to more than arrangements for public scrutiny, even if it's only a *commitment* to it. More appropriate words can be found for the moral and ethical matters involved; more words for questions of interest and motivation, and more still, if they ever get down to it, for matters of self-knowledge and self-discipline. In this instance, as in so many others, the depletion of the language actually depletes our capacity to judge, to argue, to identify possibility. This incudes the possibility that the new words are worse than useless if everyone – the honest, the dishonest and the undecided – can say with equal sincerity, as they do, that they are *committed* to them. Catchwords like this are no longer living 'words', but more like minor deities or icons the meaning of which has long been forgotten or never understood. The organisation (or cult) ritually pays obeisance and goes back to its *core business*. Much the same can be said of most (*key*) words in mission statements. If a drawing of a toad was substituted for *accountability*, and a carving of the Egyptian Goddess Sechmet was put in a corner for *transparency*, and once a year everyone renewed their *commitments* to them, nothing material would change.

'When I use a word,' Humpty Dumpty said in a rather scornful tone, 'it means just what I choose it to mean – neither more nor less.'

'The question is,' said Alice, 'whether you can make words mean so many different things.'

'The question is,' said Humpty Dumpty, 'which is to be master – that's all.'

Lewis Carroll,
Through the Looking Glass

There may be a connection between believing in these business terms and the widespread sense of entitlement that Robert Hughes, among others, has observed in our society. Some medical scientists tell us that the two most significant changes in medicine in the past century were, first, scientific development; and second, the growing belief that no mistake, inadequacy and failure should be accepted as a normal part of life. Now many of our fellow citizens, especially those in the United States – oddly, for people who believe in a Great Disposer – believe that someone or some human process is to blame. Because without blame there cannot be *closure*, and there cannot be *closure* without litigation or litigation without *closure*. By radically reducing the element of chance in life, science is chiefly responsible for this development. But the language of modern marketing and management might be adding to the trend. With all the talk of *outcomes* and *events* and *accountability* and such, it could be that these days many citizens are prone to think that most *events* are managed, and those that aren't should be: managed *transparently* in fact, into *agreed outcomes*. And if there is no such *outcome*, someone must be made *accountable*. There must be *closure*. It is very likely that the word creates the need. The most dramatic example so far appears to be the news that in some parts of the United States parents have started legal proceedings against their gynaecologists when, on reaching high school age, their children's IQs do not meet expectations.

It is odd that modern conservatives, who make so much of the cultural heritage, make very little of its single most important element, the language. Our Prime Minister, whose world-view is largely informed by English tradition, is not informed in any way that his constituents can enjoy by the English language. By his own reckoning, John Howard is the most conservative of Australian leaders; yet he is also the most modern in that platitudes are pretty well all he attempts. Every Australia Day, every Anzac Day and every day of disaster he pulls out the 'mateship' nostrum. He tells the people that 'mateship' is what defines them, as if it is *all* that defines them, all they need to know about themselves, all that he can think to say about them. In truth this is all he needs to say; it is the verbal equivalent of a physical gesture: a wave, a handshake, a wink, a nod. It will do for the occasion.

The Prime Minister did not train in managerialism and borrows only a few of its terms when he speaks to us (*core* promises and *non-core* promises, for instance); but he did say that the times would suit him and they have in every detail, including the dreary, verbless, moodless

We ourselves will be able to determine what is true and what is not.

Joseph Stalin

'We will decide who comes here and the circumstances in which they come.'

John Howard

The bourgeois prefers comfort to pleasure, convenience to liberty, and a pleasant temperature to the deathly inner consuming fire.

Hermann Hesse, *Der Steppenwolf*

cadences of the 'Generalised Life' of which he is both advocate and exemplar. Whatever the subject, he can always make it sound the same.

Dear Fellow Australian
I am writing to you because I believe you and your family should know more about some key issues affecting the security of our country and how we can all play a part in protecting our way of life . . .
 Even if the Hotline only receives one or two pieces of information that end up preventing something terrible happening, the Australian community will have made an important contribution to preventing terrorism . . .

This is from an ideological descendant of Edmund Burke.

Another ideological descendant of Burke's, Robert Menzies, could be overblown, but at least with Menzies you knew the language was alive; that he was drawing on the culture. What he could not turn into phrases of his own he took from others – from Tennyson, or Burns, or Shakespeare or Warren Hastings. Or the same Edmund Burke, who once said, 'Magnanimity in politics is not seldom the truest wisdom; a great empire and little minds go ill together.' A lack of Burkean intelligence or magnanimity might be one reason why political leaders no longer reach such memorable conclusions. Another reason is the absence of an audience for them. Modern politics is a media narrative and the last thing you need is philosophy getting in the way of it. The words that count are those that feed the story. Advisers are employed for these story-concocting skills, and speech-

Thus Belial with
  words clothed in
  reason's garb
Counselled ignoble
  ease, and
  peaceful sloth,
Not peace.
    Milton, *Paradise Lost*

Base words are
  uttered only by
  the base
And can for such
  at once be
  understood,
But noble
  platitudes: — ah,
  there's a case
Where the most
  careful scrutiny
  is needed
To tell a voice that's
  genuinely good
From one that's base
  but merely has
  succeeded.
    W.H. Auden, 'Shorts'

writers generally take their orders from them. Such gems of reflective prose as might occasionally be crafted make it into public life only when judged *on message*, or not too far off it. This means they make it hardly ever. In fact, insisting leaders stay *on message* is different only in degree from any Ministry of Propaganda dictum.

John Howard's language rarely steps far from the ordinary for the good reason that ordinary language is what people use. Very likely he also calculates that underlying the sound of ordinariness is the message of common sense, which to a literal mind means the sense of common people. From this, rather than any obvious signs of thought, modern political language gets its gravity. It is assumed that a man who speaks the language of the people will embody their wisdom. And so long as polls and elections go the way of such a person there will be plenty of commentators to say that he is tuned into the people and is much deeper than he sounds.

This is a convenient approach to political language and common in democracies. There is nothing particularly offensive about it, except that it is slumming. Compare it with Burke, whose power of thought cannot be separated from the prose in which he expresses it. In fact we cannot be sure where the thought ends and the words begin. We will never know if Burke arrived at his maxim about little minds and large empires before he wrote the sentence, or in the writing of it. We know for sure, however, that with writing it is sometimes one way and sometimes the other. Such wisdom as we have we express in language; and in language we also seek it. Which is why an impoverished language must perforce accompany impoverished thought. As Orwell said: 'It becomes ugly and inaccurate because our thoughts are foolish, but the slovenliness of our language makes it easier for us to have foolish thoughts.' Here is the Australian Prime Minister again, and remember this is not off the top of his head, but has been composed to enlighten his fellow Australians:

> Australians respect and understand the many cultures and religions that make up our society. Now, more than ever, we must work together to make sure no religion or section of our community is made to feel a scapegoat because of the actions of a small number of fanatics.

This confection touches neither the heart nor the head, and gives no sign of coming from either of those places. It's a comforter, as dead things are for some people. Lifelessness, however, does not entirely disguise the little sleights of hand. Look closely and you'll see the corpse has been tampered with. No one must be made to

I had seen nothing sacred, and all the things that were glorious had no glory and the sacrifices were like the stockyards at Chicago if nothing was done with the meat except to bury it . . . Abstract words such as glory, honour, courage, or hallow were obscene.

Ernest Hemingway,
A Farewell to Arms

feel a scapegoat. Some people, Edmund Burke for example, might have expected him to say that no one should be *made* a scapegoat. It might be an unintended slip, of course, but it sends the message – it's all right to blame them, but don't let them hear you.

At another point the letter says: *As a people we have traditionally engaged the world optimistically.* And while he's rolling on this theme: *Our open, friendly nature makes us welcome guests and warm hosts.* This rose-coloured boasting smells of some nightmare Ministry of Information. Viktor Klemperer recorded the same tone in the public language in his diary of the Nazi years in Germany. To establish as fact the myth of German superiority, the Third Reich's propagandists pursued two mutually reinforcing themes – the inferiority of certain others and the delightfulness of themselves. As a people, the Germans were culture loving, nature loving, fun loving and peace loving. The German nation and the German people were always *young*. *Sunny*, Klemperer says, was a favourite term, especially in birth and funeral notices. *As a people*, the Germans also had an *irrepressible will*, and so on. This *will* was set in direct opposition to *elites*, of the intellectual or any other kind. *Elites* were not *useful*. The categorical summaries of the German people were matched of course by equally absurd assessments of Jews, Slavs, Bolsheviks and others: and soon the language, like the regime, was rotten to its roots. We need not fear a Third Reich in Australia, but that is all the more reason for not talking in its tones.

The phrase *as a people* might not be a lie, but it smells like one. And it sits askew to the element of conservative political philosophy that opposes all attempts to categorise people by class or historic tendency, or any other conceit that will serve as an excuse for eliminating them. *The people of Australia* is not so rank because it does not carry the suggestion that some mythic or historic force unites us in our destiny. But if we must have *as a people*, then *traditionally* has to go, and not only because *optimistically* is sitting on top of it. It has to go because it is so at odds with Australian history it could be reasonably called a lie. *Traditionally* we built barriers against the world we are alleged to have engaged so *optimistically*; *traditionally* we clung to the mother country for protection against that same world; *traditionally* (if, say, Lawson, Rudd, Baynton, Furphy, Richardson, Patrick White and Ned Kelly are traditional) we took less of an optimistic view of the world than an ironic, fatalistic view of the world. The smugness of the sentence about our being lovely guests and warm hosts is so larded by fantasy and self-delusion, it transcends 'Neighbours' and becomes Edna Everage. It will occur to some readers,

What makes it so plausible to assume that hypocrisy is the vice of vices is that integrity can indeed exist under the cover of all other vices except this one. Only crime and the criminal, it is true, confront us with the perplexity of radical evil; but only the hypocrite is really rotten to the core.

Hannah Arendt,
On Revolution

surely, that it has been *our nature* recently to play very cold hosts to uninvited guests, the sort of people we don't want here, who throw their children into the sea, who are not fun-loving, welcoming, warm, sunny, etc.

Given that recent history, we might wonder if the words are as ingenuous as they sound. The thought, even the subconscious thought, might have been of a piece with Medea's 'soft talk'. Thus – *as a people* Australians are very nice; people who don't agree with this proposition are not nice people; people who are not nice are not Australian in the sense of Australians *as a people*. People who are not prepared to be Australian as a people should shut up or piss off back to where they came from.

They're just words. And to say they mean the opposite of what many people believe to be the facts is not to say it's as rotten a thing as putting *Arbeit Macht Frei* (*Work Liberates*) over the gates of Auschwitz. The Prime Minister's language is platitudinous, unctuous and deceitful. It is in bad taste.

If it is not actual propaganda, it has much in common with it. Propaganda, as John Ralston Saul says, is 'the negation of language. It destroys memory and therefore removes any sense of reality'. Abuse the language and you abuse the polity. If you construct a collective character and a mythic history and paint over them with invented virtues you also abuse the people: you demean them and deny them their own history. Myths are tempting to those who are in a position to manipulate their fellow human beings, because a myth is sacred, and what is sacred cannot be questioned. That's where their power comes from. They simplify and provide meaning without the need of reason. Marketing and advertising like them for this reason. They stifle doubt and provide relaxation and comfort. It is about here that they meet clichés, which are myths of language. But none of this, of course, is a crime against humanity.

The Americans saying they 'lost their innocence' on 11 September 2001 is a myth, and also a cliché. As Philip Roth said, the Al-Qaeda attack produced an orgy of narcissism. Narcissism naturally spawns myths: myths of character and history, of good and evil. 9/11 produced a torrent of American myths. The United States innocent? After slavery? After a Civil War? After 400 years, they're still innocent? It is like John Howard saying Australians lost *their* innocence when a lunatic ran riot and killed people at Port Arthur. Port Arthur innocent? Australia innocent? It can only be fantasy, ignorance or mischief. Or a cliché which, having lost its meaning through overuse, can be anything you want to make of it. It's one of those clichés that might as well be called a lie. It contradicts what is known, and what ought to be

Men hide behind
their clichés.
Eugene Ionesco,
Notes and Counter Notes

The true hypocrite is
the one who ceases
to perceive his
deception, the
one who lies with
sincerity.
André Gide, *Journal of
The Counterfeiters*

known; it does not help us understand a tragedy but rather diminishes it. It insults our intelligence. We may as well claim descent from Teutonic knights as claim to be innocent. As public language, it is the equivalent of airbrushing.

The trite, the obscure and the impenetrable readily become the deceitful. Instead of asking what the words mean, journalists tell us on behalf of the politician, as if the code is legitimate. At other times – it depends on the shape of the day's story – they take the most egregious nonsense at face value. Less frequently, but often enough to make you want to put a brick through the television or radio or cancel your subscription to the newspaper, they actually give points for evasive or incomprehensible language. They mean to say that the politician was clever enough to avoid the traps set for him by the Opposition or the press: but they may as well report: 'the Minister did very well at confounding his constituents today, really you have to admire the way he hides behind clichés and lies so sincerely.' Reporters who concentrated on the words would do more service to democracy. If only they would ask: 'What do you mean by *innocence*?' 'How many times can a country lose it?' 'You're an Australian – were *you* innocent?' 'Did you mean 'ignorance' – Australians lost their 'ignorance?' And when he says mateship: 'What *mateship* are you talking about there?' 'Historically speaking?' 'If it's the *tradition of mateship* as you say, do you believe in the kind of mateship that leaves out women, Asians, blacks and capitalists?' 'If it's not this tradition, what tradition is it?' 'Socialism "is just being mates," by one famous Australian account – is that the mateship you're referring to?' 'What in hell are you talking about?'

It may be that the current Prime Minister simply lacks inspiration and matches his language to this absence. It is just as likely that his blandness derives from the kind of politics they all play in these times: the poll-driven kind which demands that leaders stay *in touch* with the people, even if it means that leaders speak to us as inarticulately as the witnesses to accidents and sport we see on television. The difference between the feigned spontaneity, outrage and excitement seen in authoritarian societies and dictatorships is different solely in degree from democratic leaders who are agitated only by what agitates public opinion. More commonly, our leaders are primed to insert the bit which is the currency of political exchange – the grab or sound-bite – regardless of the consequences for language, coherence or self-respect. This creates a curious and debilitating paradox: to seem like ordinary people our leaders try not to say anything too difficult or challenging. But they must say something, partly to maintain the impression that they know something, or believe something, but mainly because that's

We can act as *if* there were a God; feel as *if* we were free; consider Nature as *if* she were full of special designs; lay plans as *if* we were to be immortal; and we find then that these words do make a genuine difference in our moral life . . .

There is no worse lie than a truth misunderstood by those who hear it.

William James,
The Varieties of Religious Experience

'The trouble with the French is they have no word for entrepreneur.'

Attributed to President George W. Bush

how it works: it's grist to the mill, so they try to say the thing that will have the most effect; a pointed, distilled sort of thing in what they reckon is language the mob will understand.

The result is that people of ordinary intelligence notice something unnatural in their gestures and something distracted in their expression, because the politician can't hide the fact that he's waiting for the chance to say what he's been primed to say, and when he gets that chance he jumps at it with unnatural haste. But because it's rehearsed it doesn't sound natural, and chances are he will add some dog-eared phrase like 'at this particular point in time' or 'a window of opportunity' or 'in terms of a window of opportunity' or 'at the end of the day', and viewers will mentally yawn as their brains struggle for oxygen, and go back to the ironing for stimulation. In his efforts to appear ordinary the politician runs the risk that ordinary people will think him inconsequential or a drongo: especially if he gets tangled between the grab he's dredging from his memory and other mental processes necessary to survive or 'think on your feet', in which event he (in this case the US President) might say something like 'You teach a child to read and he or her will be able to pass a literacy test'; or 'More and more of our imports come from overseas'; or 'I've been misunderestimated'. Or, in reaching for something grand, he might say the family is where 'our wings take dream'.

It is sad that politicians rarely attempt to put their case complete with ambiguities and contradictions; that is to say, as ordinary people generally put their cases to each other. A politician of this kind might be very popular, especially if he also had beliefs and principles. But of course this is a difficult effect to achieve when you are talking through journalists, and your advisers' words are lying like dead things in a front chamber of your brain, or you have a script in front of you which you only half believe. It's out of daily political reportage that those dying phrases come spinning slowly; and, as they do with 'Neighbours' or 'Home and Away', the people imitate them without meaning to. You'll hear them say *at this point in time* in workaday conversation, or *he would not resile* at funerals. *I am grateful for this window of opportunity to pay tribute to my father*. Or, *We will never forget the way Muriel pushed the envelope*. And then the people who write the soap operas hear it, and their characters begin to say they *will not resile* and they have *pushed the envelope*; and the language becomes less like a language and more like just what happens when you open your mouth; less like an expression of a mental process and more like gruel or reflux.

George Orwell was appalled by political language sixty years ago. He would be more appalled now. Friedrich

Nietzsche, who a hundred years ago was appalled by nearly everything, would feel vindicated *and* appalled. So too Flaubert and many others after him who contemplated mass society with dread and loathing. 'The entire dream of democracy is to raise the proletariat to the level of bourgeois stupidity', Flaubert wrote to George Sand soon after the horrors of the Paris Commune. That the bourgeoisie were stupid was clear from their pomposities and clichés. How much worse would it be when the peasants and workers started talking like that? 'Masses, numbers, are invariably idiotic', he said. How to make universal suffrage and universal education the foundations of a country without creating universal folly? Flaubert believed it could not be done; but meanwhile, he said, the prospect of it would lead to terrible revolutions like the Commune, and the reality to terrible wars (like those of the twentieth century). George Sand had a more optimistic view: she said we must fix our hopes on the essential goodness of human

I maintain that ideas are events. It is more difficult to make them interesting, I know, but if you fail the style is at fault.

Gustave Flaubert,
Letter to Louise Colet

It was said softly on a current of intense indignation . . . Each word seemed to come on a separate journey from the poet's mind to his voice, along a winding road or through an exorbitant gate.

Norman Mailer,
on seeing Robert Lowell
make a speech,
The Armies of the Night

nature (the French portion of it at least), and its capacity for love, bravery and enlightenment.

Some of our contemporaries might say that Flaubert and Sand were both wrong and that it has proved a far better thing to fix our hopes on marketing; and, better still, to create a buyer's market. So this is the era of marketing, and so we speak its language: it might be crass, but it's an improvement on the era of world war and international revolution. The argument can't be lightly dismissed. Culture, language included, always has to pay a tithe to social progress and democracy. Standards are bound to slip. It's a perpetual and necessary trade-off to keep chaos and bloodshed at bay. Vulgarity is the price of freedom. Compromise is the price of having something left at the end.

But compromise is not capitulation: each party to a compromise has something the other side needs. You show them that there is a point beyond which you won't go, and they can't without hurting themselves. That point, surely, has been reached with the language.

Orwell had his own problems with the rise of the working classes, equally despising the class system and the viciousness of mass movements to abolish it. In his famous 1946 essay, *Politics and the English Language,* and in *Animal Farm* and *1984*, he was principally concerned with the potential for language to function as a tool of totalitarian ideology. He saw this potential realised in the rhetoric of fascism and communism, in bureaucracy, managerialism and in pretentious and opinionated intellectuals. Wherever demagogues and bullies went, there also went obfuscation, pomposity and doublespeak. For Orwell, the corruption of language in public life threatened the intelligent discourse

Funding for legal aid is increasingly meeting less of the demand, but allocating additional funds on a one-off basis without a specific reason may be seen as an admission by the Government that funding is insufficient.

Department of the Prime Minister & Cabinet

on which democracy depends. Civilised society depends on the exercise of common sense, which depends on saying what we mean clearly enough for everyone of reasonable intelligence to understand. The political point follows from the general one Ben Jonson made: 'Language springs out of the most retired and inmost parts of us, and is the image of the parent of it, the mind. No glass renders a man's form and likeness so true as his speech.'

Democracy depends upon plain language. It depends upon common understanding. We need to feel safe in the assumption that words mean what they are commonly understood to mean. Deliberate ambiguities, slides of meaning, obscure, incomprehensible or meaningless words poison the democratic process by leaving people less able to make informed or rational decisions. They erode trust. Depleted language always comes with a depleted democracy: the language of undemocratic systems is proof enough of this. Where language is forced into unnatural shapes the body politic is ugly.

We need not go as far as Orwell did: not all political language is designed to make lies sound truthful and murder respectable. Political language has this tendency, but Orwell sometimes turned tendencies into absolutes. Had Lincoln followed Orwell's rules for plain language, furthermore, the Gettysburg address would have been a plain thing and only a fraction as effective; and Martin Luther King's 'I Have a Dream' speech would have to be rendered without the dream. We cannot imagine Orwell talking about 'words of interposition and nullification'. As Primo Levi says, 'clarity is a necessary but not a sufficient condition: one can be clear and boring, clear and useless, clear and untruthful, clear and vulgar . . .' Public language benefits mightily from what a contemporary observed in the young Lincoln a decade before he became President: that he had 'a curious vein of sentiment running through his thought, which is his most valuable mental attribute'. Contemporary Orwellians also need to be reminded that abolishing clichés, doublespeak and buzz words will not of itself make truth and justice flourish. But to aim towards this happy state (even to *benchmark* it) is sensible because it might do good: as much good as, for instance, reforming the upper house of a state parliament or abolishing the House of Lords, and with less chance of unanticipated strife.

Each week on Australian television, John Clarke begins his comment on the week's news by telling us he is someone who plainly he is not. Beginning with this most fundamental deceit, his conversations with Bryan Dawe distil the public language to nothing. After three

But words in their influence are subtle and delicate beyond all things known to man, and the least change in them when they are in company, or the least addition to that company, cannot but entail a change of meaning: a change, that is, in their complete effect, on the mind and spirit of the reader.

Walter de la Mare,
Stories from the Bible

minutes there is only a lunatic stalemate, as if this is all there is in public life, before the relief of the empty gestures: 'Thank you for appearing on the program.' 'Always a pleasure.' Corrupted language is an indispensable source of humour. Groucho and Chico Marx got half their jokes from corrupted language. It is one of comedy's oldest routines to stretch the language to the point of breaking, or mimic those who do it naturally. But no comic could do much better than George W. Bush, the man who has some claim to be the most powerful the world has ever known, when he says, just like Chico: 'He can't take the high horse and then claim the low road'; or throttles his Saviour's message into ersatz narcissism, 'We must all hear the universal call to like your neighbour just like you like to be liked yourself'. Chico might have said that too.

All totalitarian regimes, regardless of their ideological origin, pervert language to delude, intimidate and mystify their subjects. They also take the humour out of it, even when the circumstances are laughable. Stalin sent his erstwhile comrades to their deaths confessing ludicrously concocted crimes, and countless intelligent people were persuaded to believe them. What is it that torture and brainwashing try to extract? Words. They need the word as well as the corpse. If words define reality, you cannot control the one without controlling the other. This surely helps explain Stalin's obsession with writers (and musicians), and even occasional splenetic outbursts against them in open societies where casual indifference is normal. In the so-called culture wars of recent years an effort has been made to ignore them pointedly. Conservative politicians, including many on the Labor side, have discovered words to label amorphous categories of malcontents as irrelevant or stupid. Words like *elite*, *chattering classes* and *café latte* are insipid in their usual environment but, like certain animals and chemical compounds, become poisonous and destructive in another one.

There is an old vein of anti-intellectualism in this, and another one of scapegoating. And a third insists that artists, like their distant cousins in universities, accept managerial or *main game* classifications. Writers and painters now work in an arts *industry*, where they can be expected to do what people do in other industries: namely, *add value*, *continuously improve* and become *world class*. The trend has something to do with the globalisation of the culture, and something else about it is endemic to post-colonial societies keen to prove that they can cut it in the wider world. But managerial terms reveal a managerial *ideology* at work: a set of ideas refined into a self-reinforcing belief system. In this case, weirdly, the ideology managerialism most resembles is a

The shot-gun was not resorted to. Masked men did not ride over the country at night intimidating voters; but there was a firm feeling that a class existed in every State with a sort of divine right to control public affairs. If they could not get this control by one means they must by another.

Ulysses S. Grant,
Personal Memoirs

debased Marxism. Isolating artists and intellectuals, or offering them a choice between frightening, often fatal isolation and fatally compromised incorporation, is an old and sinister theme of history with its nadir in the Soviet Union. Not that the language of management leads by even circuitous roads to the Gulag; but nor does it open the way to all the virtues of an open society. Similarly, dubbing everyone whose reading of history leads them to conclusions different from the preferred ones *black-armband historians*; channelling frustrations felt by the politically powerless to the *politically correct*; isolating *chattering classes* and *elites* from a pretended mainstream – all these and many terms of political abuse are common and inevitable in democracies – and all have parallels in tyrannies.

Australia is not proto-fascist (even if Norman Mailer insists that our major ally is), but it is wise just the same to keep an eye on politicians for signs they are traducing not just opposing politicians, but constituents whose thinking doesn't suit. Watch how, in lieu of actual exile, they are labelled 'illegitimate'. When the words are suspicious, go after them, insist they tell us what they mean. Go after the *meaning* of the words. And if the speakers say they are the kind who call things as they see them, that they don't mince words, and call a spade a spade if not a bloody shovel, go after them even harder. They're often the worst liars of the lot.

We citizens have intuition, natural scepticism and powers of analysis to go on, but we still rely on facts and in the end have to trust our leaders to tell us what is actually the case. Whether it's a lie, a half-truth, a weasel word, a banality, a buzz word or a cliché, if we are misled by it our rights are reduced in proportion. Words are bullets. They are also good for smothering, strangling and poisoning, and for hiding murderous intentions from your victims (and sometimes from yourself). The Nazis called their plans to exterminate millions of people by industrial means *the final solution*, which was no less a lie than informing families of concentration camp inmates that their son or brother or father or mother had died *while attempting to escape*. Every war throws up new corruptions (*wastage* from the First World War, *collateral damage* from World War II, *deconfliction*, *attrited* and *degraded* from Iraq) and at the same time, as Hemingway said, they make old words like *honour* and *glory* sound obscene.

George W. Bush's words are generally less menacing and more laughable, but they live in the same murky region where language is broken and remoulded into bizarre shapes to satisfy the needs of power. So we should be concerned when the world's most powerful man makes speeches of this kind.

METHOD – The bird, if small, may be cut down the back, and flattened and cooked like a spatchcock of chicken; if large, it is better divided into joints. In either case the whole of it must be brushed over with warm fat, and seasoned with salt and a very little cayenne, before grilling. (Pheasant grilled.)

Mrs Beeton's Everyday Cookbook

'I went into a mode of self-preservation.'

Footballer,
Fox Footy Channel

I know America wants reconciliation and unity. I know Americans want progress. And we must seize this moment and deliver. Together, guided by a spirit of common sense, common courtesy and common goals, we can unite and inspire the American citizens.

Together we will make all our public schools excellent, teaching every student of every background and every accent, so that no child is left behind . . .

Together we will address some of society's deepest problems one person at a time, by encouraging the good hearts and good works of the American people . . .

I have faith that with God's help we as a nation will move forward as one nation, indivisible.

To which one can only say, that if God helps it's a reasonable hope to have. But if God can read between the lines, he's not going to fall for what an earlier generation of American commentators might have called *bomfog* or *flapdoodle* or *tomfoolery* or *hokum* or so much *hornswaggle*. 'All our schools excellent'? 'Every student'? 'One person at a time'? With the greatest respect, we don't think so. Not even with common courtesy behind us. It's not just the disingenuousness, the outrageous promises that insult our common sense; it's the tired prose: the dead words, *encouraging, empowering, reconciliation, unity, together, no child is left behind. Together we will address . . .* Perhaps that's what they do in Texas. *Yeehah! Let's go addressing!*

These lists have all the moral force of the copy on a cereal packet, and in much the same way combine the ultra-mundane ('These oatflakes contain carbo-hydrates . . .' What oats don't?) and the outrageous ('. . . to get you through the day'. You mean we won't make it without them?) Add niacin, riboflavin and Vitamins A, B, and C and you'll get through your day just like the lovely iron man breasting the tape in the picture gets through his. 'Together' is the carbohydrate of this speech; common courtesy, common sense etc., are, if you like, the vitamins and minerals. The cereal advertising turns a need (nutrition) into a want (health and beauty), for which read hopeless desire. The political speech works on the same formula. The breakfast table and the podium: marketing triumphs at both venues. And not only in Texas. The speech might as well have been written in Canberra or Wellington or London, Labor or conser-vative. Vapidity is an *international* political language.

US Presidents are more than ciphers; but watching them you wonder if the essential purpose of their existence is to read the speeches. The speeches are in the main confections of American myths and ideals, and this does indeed make the President something of a cipher. Sometimes he is in Frontierland, sometimes Tomorrowland. He is at different times a cowboy, a sheriff, a general, a statesman, a down-home all American boy: John Wayne, Teddy Roosevelt, George Patton, Huck Finn: log cabin to White House: Harvard Business School to White House. Remember the Alamo! Remember the Twin Towers! The prose can be grandiloquent, but it is always predictable.

> We will not tire, we will not falter, and we will not fail . . . I will not yield; I will not rest; I will not relent in any way in this struggle for freedom and security for the American people.

A Presidential speech has this much in common with country and western music – we know what chord is coming next and what words: *alone* will follow *phone*, *you* will follow *do* or *true*; *heart*, *apart*, and so on until you feel you've been baptised in warm treacle. Yet, because he is reading complete and shapely sentences, the Presidential performance is

'It contains a misleading impression, not a lie. It was being economical with the truth.'
Robert Armstrong,
UK public servant during Spycatcher trial

We have got to exert ourselves a little to keep sane and call things by the names other people call them by.
George Eliot,
Middlemarch

invested with a sort of old-world grace, a period quality which in a kitsch culture suggests the authentic past, even the eternal. And the ghosts of the dead it brings forth, and all those American dreams and everything that made the country great, and everything the enemies of freedom want to destroy, combine irresistibly with the flag draped behind him and millions of viewers find that their hands have crept over hearts that are beating so much stronger. Such patriotic clichés our own leaders now try manfully to replicate with flags and humbug about mateship, the national character and Gallipoli.

Public language has its origins in power: in the executive decrees of priests, rulers and their subalterns. It is the language of the mighty – or the meretricious – mediated for us by democratic sentiment or the perceived need to take account of it. Thus when George W. Bush delivers his State of the Union address to Congress he veers strategically between the unfettered belligerence of a real emperor whose might is unquestionable, and the sanctimony of a phony one whose might derives in some measure from the people. He says, *We will prevail*, not *I will prevail*, and if the effect is to make many viewers suspect that by *we* he means himself, Dick Cheney, Donald Rumsfeld and a handful of unseen others, it's still held to be better than the egotistical *I*.

Balancing your ego with your constituents' egos is one of the essential arts of leadership, and because language is the main mediator in this, it is a daily concern for speechwriters. Here is Hillary Clinton adjusting the balance in the modern Democratic way.

Was he free? Was
he happy? The
question was
absurd:
Had anything been
wrong, we should
certainly have
heard.

W.H. Auden,
'The Unknown Citizen'

Man is most
comforted by
paradoxes.

G.K. Chesterton,
Introduction to the
Book of Job

I think that in everyday ways, how you treat your disappointments, and whether you forgive the pain that others cause you, and frankly, to acknowledge the pain you cause to others, is one of the biggest challenges we face as we move into the next century.

Frankly, another big challenge as we move into the next century is avoiding cliché. I think, speaking of everyday ways, we could begin by not saying *challenge*. It only *seems* necessary.

We need not argue with Hillary Clinton's sentiments. Countless magazines and daytime television are expressly created for the moments when you feel you must go public with them. But if she (along with much of the English-speaking world) were not so habituated to the word *challenge* she might have taken her idea to some less bizarre conclusion, and left us less worried about a world run by American Democrats. Without *challenge* playing fridge to her magnet, she might have said only that we will be happier when we learn to cope with pain and disappointment. This at least gets it in proportion, even if it is not much different to saying we will be happier when we are happier. But that's where solipsism takes you and it's an important part of the economy these days. Without the cant word, *challenge*, drawing her on, she might not have felt compelled to rank coping with unhappiness among the *biggest challenges we face as we move into the new century*: along with other challenges like Africa, the Middle East and nuclear weapons, we presume. And she might have thought just long enough to remember that old Job was coping with pain and disappointment well before daytime television got hold of it.

Orwell might groan; but Nietzsche would yawn. Nietzsche had less faith in people of reasonable intelligence: democracy was a political system calculated to make the intelligent minority subject to the will of the stupid. Of course, then, the language of democracy is impoverished and corrupted – or moronic, to use a favourite word of Nietzsche's most famous American disciple, H. L. Mencken. Moronic like the morons democracy puts in charge. Nietzsche would very likely say the language of democracy merely reflects the *nature* of democracy; the corruptions of language are not aberrations, any more than electing mediocrities to high office is an aberration. When George W. Bush speaks, we're getting the real thing. It is the mass we are hearing – or, more precisely, language that has been programmed for their level of intelligence and interest. When the Texan unfurls his vision in chaotic prose, it is just as Nietzsche (and Flaubert and all the others) said it would be.

The question is not easily settled, but the trend to a globalised culture dominated by a great mass democracy of unprecedented power in the world, including the power to infantalise it, might favour the Nietzschean view. So might local imitations of American-style poll-driven politics, the triumph of free market economics, managerialism and other species of philistine self-interest including the universal narcissism that is an inevitable by-product of a market-driven society and necessary to keep it running. If Nietzsche is right, attempts to arrest the decline of language are equivalent to arresting history, which is to say a waste of time – one such, indeed, as only a moron could conceive. We can give up the wait for an inspiring word from our leaders and look forward to everyone talking like a *Knowledge Manager*.

Knowledge Managers talk like this: *frameworks . . . based upon reflection in action, pragmatic real world systems implementations, as well as theory and practice defining research conducted over the*

Our procedures in respect of the audit of the concise financial report included testing that the information in the concise financial report is consistent with the full financial report, and examination on a test basis, of evidence supporting the amounts, discussion and analysis, and other disclosures which were not directly derived from the full financial report.

Financial report

It is conceivable that the language of the future world will also be the purely functional means of communication that for the natural scientist it already is today.

Jean Amery,
'How Much Home Does a Person Need?'

past two decades. They talk like this because *Knowledge Management*:

> . . . caters to the critical issues of organisational adaption, survival, and competence in face of increasingly discontinuous environmental changes . . . Essentially it embodies organisational processes that seek synergistic combination of data and information processing capacity of information technologies and the creative and innovative capacity of human beings.

Let's defer to the bottom line: let's try to quantify it. What costs the culture more: the theft of a Matisse or rare manuscript, or rafts of consultants telling the institutions in which they are housed that they need *structural envisioning*? To *envision structurally* is to:

Build structural options by activity/process, output and customer

Select a model to explore/develop process/output combination

Refine structural concept, develop notional function hooks for key processes and outputs.

(Later they intend *to test the structural concept by assigning the accountabilities to* [the] *notional functional hooks*, but doubtless that is another story, and probably will be billed separately). The Matisse and the manuscript at least had worth while they existed; they were seen, remembered, copied. But what is the worth of *structural envisioning*? And what has it to do with conserving and displaying manuscripts and paintings?

Far from being sued or gaoled for this, the consultants ask for and invariably receive very large amounts of money. Politicians who confound us in the same way – who say, for instance that they are *committed* to a library or a gallery when for all that means they may as well face in its direction and blow their noses – also go free; many of them indeed with a Gold Pass and abundant superannuation. Doubtless the business, bureaucratic and political classes would all be inclined to defend themselves by pointing to the success of the national economy, or its corporate equivalent, the *bottom line*. Up against the wall, were we ever able to get them there, they might even try the one about their own success being proof against the allegations. Why would they pay me this much if I wasn't doing something right? A professional wrestler would say the same. The well-rewarded have *always* said it. Press them hard and they will tell you that the present *scenario*, including the BMW, is the work of God.

'I imagine the sorts of children who would be thrown would be those who could be readily lifted and tossed without any objection from them.'

Philip Ruddock,
Herald Sun,
9 October 2001

'I don't want people like that in Australia. Genuine refugees don't do that . . .'

John Howard,
Herald Sun,
8 October 2001

Should boat people who throw children into the sea be accepted into Australia as refugees?

Herald Sun, 'Have Your Say', 8 October 2001

The art of connecting words creates shades of meaning. This makes it an art of deep importance; because a shade of meaning is as consequential as a fundamental difference. I don't need to be utterly wrong; being slightly wrong will mislead just as well. If I say 'Ms Kidman is little short of sensational in the role', it means one thing; but by adding nothing more than an *a*, to make, 'Ms Kidman is a little short of sensational in the role', I make my meaning suddenly more obscure, ambiguous, possibly ironic, mischievous or even contemptuous. If I say *axis of evil* when, for all the proofs of evil, there is no evidence of an *axis* existing, I am as likely to cause as much confusion as if I had said *axle of evil* or *praxis of evil* or something even more ridiculous. If I say *nests of evil*, or *governments with evil in common*, the confusion will likely take a different form and, because it is a more accurate description, it is likely there will be less of it. It is not the context but the words that shape the meaning here. Each word is a weapon of a different kind and wounds in different ways.

Plainly the provocation is also in who says the words and how. It helps if it is someone with a claim to wisdom, for example. But then someone who is wise might not choose what, by any definition, is the wrong word – *axis*. Someone concerned about shades of meaning – and concerned about the consequences of getting them wrong – might not choose *evil*. *Evil* is a word without shades, which means the accuser best be without sin. And since the word is absolute, there is risk in using it selectively. It might seem to sanction evil beyond the *axis*, while those within it conclude they're being picked on and wonder if the words have less to do with evil than with certain strategic ambitions. A wise person, or a cautious or disinterested person, might not say *axis of evil*; but a cunning person might. A cunning person might say *evil* as often as is necessary to make him feel good, or his constituents feel both good about themselves and fond of him for making them feel that way. For the same kind of reasons the word *illegals* was attractive to people who wanted to prevent refugees landing in Australia. *Queue jumpers* worked the same way. The refugees had broken no Australian law, and there had been no queue for them to jump. But the terms were not intended to describe reality; rather to twist and conceal it in a way that would incite contempt and fear. It's words like these, as Norman Mailer says, that get to be addictive: you press the button once and it seems to work, so you press it again and again. That's why in a democracy it pays to listen carefully: don't read their lips, read their words.

To be useful in political language is not the same thing as being clear. In fact it's very often

In Anthony Swofford's memoir, *Jarhead*, he describes coming upon trenches of dead Iraqis: 'Some of the corpses in the bunkers are hunched over, hands covering their ears, as though they'd been waiting in dread. Many seemed to have died not from shrapnel, but concussion, and dried, discoloured blood gathers round their eyes, and noses and mouths . . .'
He is describing the effects of the Daisy Cutter, the smaller version of the Massive Ordinance Air Blast that the US now uses.
That language is not degraded.
Russell Smith,
'The New Newsspeak',
New York Review of Books

the opposite. *Compassionate conservatism* (a relative term if ever there was one) has proved useful to the President of the United States and the Republican Party, but it is three years since he first used it and still no one knows what it means. By the time this book is published, quite possibly no one will be saying *moral clarity*. Socrates, St Augustine and Kant, among others who fretted all their lives about the subject, may rest easier in their graves. *Moral clarity* is not so much an idea as a buzz word: a *you're in/you're out* word, as *liberal* is in modern America and *liberalistic* was in Hitler's Germany. It is an intellectual way of saying, 'Just do it!' and watching to see who jumps. The enemies of *moral clarity* are waverers and bleeding hearts, who are, the argument goes, *moral relativists*. *Moral relativists* are, if not friends of terrorists and rogues, less patriotic and American than Americans possessed of *moral clarity*. *Moral relativists* are closely related to *cultural relativists* and it is *cultural relativists*, of course, who tie the country in knots pleading multiculturalism and the rights of non-English-speakers. This is not to say it is patriotic to despise all forms of relativism: if you did that you might be less inclined to favour *low-yield* nuclear weapons which are relative, surely, to where you're standing when they go off. It is impossible to be an imperial power – or even a politician (God-fearing or not) – without exercising some degree of *moral relativism*. It's very difficult to fight a war without exercising it, and quite impossible to market one. The problem is apparent in terms like *humane war*, *surgical strike* and *smart bomb*: they are *relatively* humane, surgical and smart. *Weapons of Mass Destruction* is another relative term: some WMD are much more destructive

'The British
Government has
learned that Saddam
Hussein recently
sought significant
quantities of
uranium from
Africa.'

George W. Bush,
State of the Union, 2003

And he used an
interesting word:
'moral'. 'It just isn't
moral to play with
our children's
future,' he said. It
was used in passing,
no special emphasis,
but I saw Jack
Stanton flinch.

Anonymous,
Primary Colors:
A Novel of Politics

than others, and some not called
WMD are plainly capable of
causing mass destruction. Never-
theless, *moral clarity* is an extraordinarily useful term and it is a
wonder someone did not think of it
earlier: especially someone living in
a country founded by Puritans.

In April 2003 we heard less of
moral clarity but *vital role* was
everywhere. We heard of the *vital
role* of the United Nations in Iraq.
The *vital role* of Australia in
Iraq. The *vital role* of the Iraqis
in Iraq. No one, however, seemed to
know what it meant, or if they did
they weren't saying. Thus our leaders
insist on *moral clarity*, but not verbal
clarity. It is puzzling that the same
people can be confident about a
subject on which some of history's
greatest minds cannot agree, yet confounded by the meaning of a simple
phrase of their own making.

We need not waste time puzzling about it. In modern media-
driven politics, words are chosen
less for their meaning than for
their ability to do the job. In business and politics words are not so
much uttered as *implemented*.
With *moral clarity* they implement

a mace: with *vital role* a shield or smokescreen. Pursue them further (as if anybody does!) and they will implement a red herring, a snow job, a complete furphy or the next question.

When her long career was over, the soprano Magda Olivero said that the notes she sang divinely were not just notes but 'expressions of the soul'. Each time she went on stage, she said, 'A halo opened . . . a magic halo. I would enter this magic halo and only leave it at the end of the opera.' When the President of the United States stands before the US Congress to deliver the State of the Union one might expect him to experience something similar. He doesn't have the music, but the moment is his for commanding: a magnificent stage, a captive audience, the most sophisticated audio equipment and teleprompters, a script that has been honed and rehearsed for weeks. It is a moment of pure power. It is the rhetorical moment: the moment when traditionally the politician becomes the artist reaching into his own deep sensibilities to inspirit or enlighten the thoughts and feelings of his audience. Or share them. Or confirm them. This rhetoric is also called leadership. It is – or was – the means by which leaders create a public frame of reference for events. To lead successfully is to have the people perceive things through that frame. Today the frame is called the *story* or the *message*.

But watching Presidents in this most operatic of political settings, hardly ever are we moved. It's the lack of music, of course, and even if they could perform the dramatic equivalent of Callas in *Tosca*, we are suspicious if not downright hostile to politicians who use operatic techniques. We've seen the images of Hitler, and if one of our own tries that sort of thing we want him tied up and

'Who could not be moved by the sight of that poor, demoralised rabble, outwitted, outflanked, outmanoeuvred by the US military? Yet, given time, I think the press will bounce back.'

James Baker, *quoted in the Guardian, March 1991*

Military historians should concern themselves less with some manoeuvre or strategy from generals: If you can discover how a young unknown man inspired a ragged, mutinous, half-starved army and made it fight, how he gave it the energy and momentum to march and fight as it did, how he dominated and controlled generals older and more experienced than himself, then you have learned something.

Sir Archibald Wavell

carted away at once. In the end it may be that the words are overwhelmed by the performing moment. We can hear a singer – any kind of singer – sing a song a hundred times and if it's a good song, or it has some significance in our life, it will move us. Perhaps it's the 'vein of sentiment' in them. But when we watch a political leader perform today, the words come in a supporting role to all the other forces enlisted to serve the message.

The media conspire in it by asking if he looked the part; if his timing was good and if he sounded confident. They also ask if the politics were smart; will it play well in the marginals – was he *hunting where the ducks are*, as the Americans say. Had Lincoln been asked those questions after Gettysburg, his speech might easily have been called a failure. Policy – what he says he'll *do* – is also an important measure, but only one of several. The language of the speech is separated from the idea, which is another reason it might come over as ventriloquism, and why these days it is customary to think of rhetoric as 'empty' –

133

not as argument but as gloss; or trickery. 'Long on rhetoric, short on substance', our commentators will say of a 'Gettysburg-style' address – as they would have said about Lincoln's original. 'A grab bag of promises', they might say of a policy speech; and declare that the politician had failed to inspire or effectively pitch his program. And if he attempts this, they will say it was a 'blatant' pitch to some part of the populace, a pitch so *transparent* in fact, that no voter is ever going to fall for it. Next time our politician tries to score on all fronts, and only adds to the record yet another rhetorical henhouse. The lesson is: words cut off from the impulse that created them are often as good as dead. They are so far from being 'expressions of the soul', the greatest prima donna could not save them.

Much as we would like to hear them we need something more from politics than 'expressions of the soul'. Politics is an argument; it engages the intellect as well as the emotions. When only the emotions (or the prejudices, or the fantasies, or myths and ideology) are engaged, we smell deceit. We think the chances are we're being fooled or short-changed; and if we don't think it, chances are we have been. The words our leaders use are the base material of an honest polity and a good society. Language is fundamental to democracy because, once we've done with the hoopla and analysed the facial tics and gestures, the words are all we have to go on.

That is why we should not vote for any politician who says, for instance, *there are no quick fixes* more than three times a year. Punish her for banality and the contempt for us that it implies.

Attack the words and we might get closer to what

If the particular crime committed in Ireland a century ago could not happen now, it is not because present-day statesmen are an improvement on their predecessors. It is because the common conscience of mankind no longer allows statesmen to live up to their principles.

AJP Taylor, *'Genocide'*, *Essays in English History*

we need from them: evidence of a mind, ideas, arguments, signs of conscientious effort and disinterested reasoning, a hint of imagination. We want to see what they are offering us and what they offer the country. By this we mean the opposite of platitudes, the sausage meat of politics: we mean what in the way of leadership, management, government. If they can turn loaves into flatheads, good; but we will be satisfied to see some evidence that they understand their duties and our lives. We like to see a sign that they know what irritates us, what we hope for and what makes us despair. We want to know if they 'get it'. That does not mean we only want to hear calculated echoes of what we the public think; we would also be grateful for something to think *about*. There is idealism in this, but democracy is an ideal and it needs idealism. And critics of ideals. It needs the arguments. This makes the public language fundamental.

There is an argument that goes, as the public realm declines so must the public language. An empty public realm means an empty public language in proportion.

People living in affluent free market economies have no need or desire for visionary or charismatic leaders, or for the ennobling, inspiring, binding rhetoric with which they build their influence. Who needs a narcissist to lead in a narcissistic society? Who will respect power when everyone's *empowered*? When there is a remote control in every room with a television, and a host of channels, which ambitious leader is going to pass up style for substance, a cliché for a complex sentence, an image for an argument?

Politicians are now so conscious of the boundaries of safety and opportunity, they speak as if what they are describing has been decided in advance of them: as indeed it has, by polls and focus groups. They say what the people want and not what they will do. If being human is to believe passionately, to be wilful, funny and powerful, they make a great effort not to be human. At the extreme end of this moderation politics appears to have collided with what the postmodern calls 'the death of the author'. There are states in the Commonwealth of Australia governed by people of such little apparent personality or belief, they seem to exist only to fulfil the basic requirement of democracy that the media and the people have someone to judge. We no longer see or hear politicians whose words spring directly from conviction, or in whom power obviously lives. These things, the realities of politics, are kept out of sight. Writing, Victor Serge said, should be 'a testimony to the vast flow of life through us'. Serge was a revolutionary, but his belief fits well enough with all democratic sentiment. When did you last hear 'testimony to the vast flow of life' in the public language?

Print is the sharpest and the strongest weapon of our party.
Joseph Stalin

A great writer is, so to speak, a second government in his country. And for that reason no regime has ever loved great writers, only minor ones.
Alexander Solzhenitsyn,
The First Circle

While the polls distil the popular position to bloodless caution, it is possible that the people could stand a little more excitement. It seems incredible that since 11 September 2001 no leader has uttered words that will ring forever in our minds, or even for a year or two. True, there's no Lincoln among them, or a Kennedy, a Roosevelt or even a Clinton. But our leaders might look elsewhere for inspiration their imagination can't provide. They might look in the language. We should never miss an opportunity to quote things by others: as Proust said; they are 'always more interesting than those one thinks up oneself'. There has not been so much as a 'Farewell sweet prince . . .', or 'Why should a horse, a dog, a rat have breath . . .' Not these days: our leaders think up nothing and look up nothing.

And yet people like good words. Play them Martin Luther King and they will listen and you can be sure in any audience of a dozen one or two will brush away tears. This is at least partly because King understood how like a song a speech can be. But then someone reading them the Gettysburg address, or George Washington's speech when he stepped down from the Presidency, or Roosevelt's on becoming President in the middle of the Depression, will also move people, because the language and the thoughts are powerful.

Here is Roosevelt's sinewy inauguration address in 1933, very different in style to President Bush's 2001 address to Congress, and bearing a very different message about fear.

This is pre-eminently the time to speak the truth, the whole truth, frankly and boldly. Nor need we shrink from honestly facing conditions in our country today . . . So first of all let me assert my firm belief that the only thing we have to fear is fear itself – nameless, unreasoning, unjustified terror which paralyses needed efforts to convert retreat into advance.

It is not particularly original prose, but all the words are strung on the same taut thread: when he wants to emphasise a thought, like the thought about 'fear itself', he tightens the thread, and it resonates like a guitar string. You can't avoid the meaning and once you've heard it, you remember it. Words *can* be like notes, like expressions of the soul. They can make our hair stand up, they can lift our understanding to a higher plane, make us see things differently. They can inspire love and hope. You can see it happen before your eyes. Words can create a magic halo. But they have to have some thought or sentiment attached; and, like notes, be skilfully arranged.

'When the President does it, that means that it is not illegal.'
Richard Nixon

What is truth? said jesting Pilate, and would not stay for an answer.
Francis Bacon, *Of Truth*

When people make speeches they attempt an embrace. They say to their audience, 'you and me both': we are for all practical purposes the same. Martin Luther King did it in sentences that swept his audience across the United States – 'from the prodigious hilltops of New Hampshire . . . to the curvaceous slopes of California', and many places in between. FDR did it, comparing the troubles of Americans in 1933 with 'the perils which our forefathers conquered'. Pericles, Lincoln and Mark Antony all did it in their own way. It's a universal device: it says we are all one, with one profound inheritance, and one ideal to live up to. Speechmaking is an exercise in welding people together by welding them to whatever it is they have in common, be it their landscape, their ancestors, their ambitions, even their language.

Politicians rarely get to make speeches as far-reaching as Martin Luther King at the Lincoln Memorial; but they can say similar things when they open a pre-school in an outer suburb, or a medical centre in a country town. They can talk about the suburban frontier, that most common of Australian experiences. They can link a new housing estate to the nation's history, and the nation's values and the Australian dream. They can do the same in the country town, except here they will talk about rural *values*, and community *values*, and quite possibly the *values* of mateship and sticking together. And not for nothing our politician will be seen soon afterwards patting cows and dogs and babies – because, if he got his words right, that is what he has just done with the people. He has stroked them, comforted them, bonded with them; told them that far from being forgotten they are a priceless asset, part of the heroic national story and frequently on his mind.

Satire, Jonathan Swift said, is a kind of glass wherein the beholder sees everyone but himself. A political leader – the very opposite of a satirist – constructs a speech as the very opposite kind of mirror: one wherein, he hopes, every beholder will see himself. The idea has something in common with Proust's observation that, 'In reading every reader is, while he is reading, the reader of his own self'. Every listener to a political speech is asking: Does he know who I am? What I think? What I need? What I am entitled to? This is the politician's berley: if he has a feel for them he can strew it on the water, watch them rise and catch them with his idea. But it takes more than a photograph with the local manager or the netball team. It amounts to more than just being seen there. Some imaginative effort is required, some knowledge of the local landscape and some understanding of history. It requires a bit of psychological insight.

To be more than an exercise in spin, a mere gesture, or a confection for the media, democratic politics needs the language. It is one thing to get us eating from the palms of their hands, another to nourish us.

> To find my home in one sentence, concise,
> as if hammered in metal.
>
> Czeslaw Milosz

WHEREAS EARLIER GENERATIONS WERE inclined to quote from poets, the present one employs them. *Wordsmiths*, they call them. The present Prime Minister (and a minister in the government before his) engaged the poet Les Murray to write an Oath or Allegiance, a burst of rhetoric by which the people might forever know themselves. They engaged him less as a poet and more as a plumber. They employed him literally, prosaically. They never felt obliged to dip into his poems. He was just another consultant to be called on for his skills, or just as likely to add a bit of class that for ten times the price McKinsey's could not come up with. It is the last word in specialisation, surely, when the country's unofficial poet laureate is treated as just another expert.

Implicit in the recruiting of wordsmiths to the political and corporate cause is the notion that writing is an activity distinct from thinking. In fact every writer knows that it's in the writing that many ideas are formed. (This may be one reason why many brilliant writers are not brilliant talkers.) The phony separation of the two facilities might rescue public language from the *absolute* pits, but it leaves the travesty untouched and spreading. Government and corporate powers go on thinking in what they imagine are the only ways for governments and corporations to think, and employ writers to tinker with the words. The next generation will marvel that there was a time when business and government were able to think and write at the same time.

In the modern public service, the career of John Maynard Keynes might have terminally stalled; not because he was a Keynesian in a non-Keynesian age, but because he wrote in a style that intelligent lay people understood, and even enjoyed. It is even possible that had he written as they write nowadays he would not have been able to think his way to a Keynesian position. Something similar can be assumed of Lincoln's Gettysburg speech, which in the end is a poem. Peggy Noonan, Ronald Reagan's speechwriter, famously amended Gettysburg in the way a team of Washington advisers might have. Virtually nothing remained of the poetry or the substance – nothing, at least, to live beyond the next day's news. A modern Australian version would fare no better.

One hundred and two years ago our great grandfathers and mothers implemented a new nation (under God) with a commitment to Australia, Britain, and mateship, access and equity. Today we're confronting a challenge to see whether, hopefully, a country with these commitments and some new ones to the United

States and rich multicultural diversity will still be there at the end of the day.

The difference between this and previous ages seems to be that in ours the same clichés find their way everywhere. No class or category of work or wealth confines them. They defy educational and occupational barriers. What you hear on daytime television you will also hear from a senator, from a chief executive, a high school student. Not long ago the word *customers* was generally understood – with a few variations – to mean purchasers or clients, people who took their custom to a shop or some other kind of commercial establishment. Now libraries and universities have customers, just as the CIA and McDonald's have customers. Do not be surprised if one day you hear an American general talk of *enemy customers* – of *attriting* them, quite possibly.

Flaubert's *Dictionary of Received Ideas* was a compendium of clichés, 'idiotic' bourgeois terms and social responses. No doubt it was clever when it was written, but

---

Hackneyed phrases . . . The purpose with which these phrases are introduced is for the most part that of giving a fillip to a passage that might be humdrum without them . . . but their true use when they come into the writer's mind is as danger signals; he should take warning that when they suggest themselves it is because what he is writing is bad stuff, or it would not need such help; let him see to the substance of his cake instead of decoration with sugarplums.

Fowler and Fowler,
A Dictionary of Modern English Usage

now it is altogether too clever. A politician who used the clichés mocked by Flaubert would dazzle us with originality. Take the word *paradox*. He writes: *always originates on the Boulevard des Italiens between two puffs on a cigarette*. Very good indeed; but what we would give for a public figure to recognise a paradox, or a dilemma, or even a little ambiguity and invite us to share in the puzzle. Flaubert quotes the clichéd use of *gaiety* (*always preceded by 'frantic'*). When did we last hear the word used? Is there a significant public figure we can even imagine using it? Or *felicity*? Or *Abelard*. Or *odalisk*? He says of the word *hard – invariably as iron*. But no one says *hard as iron* any more. They say *hard decisions* which is to say uncomfortably difficult. A hard decision is closely related to *there are no quick fixes*.

Managerial language rarely evokes the physical world, another reason there is no life in it. Where Flaubert heard nauseating condescension we might hear something genuine: *Farm workers – what would we do without them?* There are now too few farm workers to be worth a politician's time. If, however, a politician said, *What would we do without you?* to workers in a call centre or some other modern workplace, he might move their hearts. The words would impress people who caught it on the evening news. Some viewers might even shed tears, because they are used to hearing people say, *we value your contribution; we appreciate your commitment; you have our gratitude going forward*. After you've heard these words a hundred times, *What would we do without you?* sounds direct, heartfelt, human, generous.

Flaubert mocks it, but how much happier we would be if our bank said *a sword of Damocles* was hanging

In judging a regime it is very important to know what it finds amusing.

Palmiro Togliatti

First I'm reading it; but also it is intruding, obtruding, nudging, pushing, whispering to me about things I know about my own life, and that's what makes it work as a drama.

Dennis Potter,
Potter on Potter

over us; or that they had been in a *dark and impenetrable thicket*; or that a swallow was a *harbinger of spring*? They might be clichés, but when you're used to hearing about the *integral aspects of our medium term commitment*, they don't sound like clichés. They sound colourful and gay. Hearing them might make you whistle for a week. But when did you last hear someone whistling? Possibly in Ireland; but ten years ago before the modern economic miracle and Sony turned the Irish people's need for Walkmen and Discmen into wants.

Ireland remains a place where there is pleasure in hearing public language spoken. It is a pocket of resistance in the empire of the English language. On the upholstery of Aer Lingus planes, slices of *Ulysses* and poems have been embroidered. William Butler Yeats's 'The Lake Isle of Innisfree' spills over the back of the seat in front of you – truly a beautiful arrangement of words. With the plane going down, what would you like to enter your head in the moment before you realise death is coming at a thousand miles an hour, Hugh Grant or:

> I will arise and go now, for always night and day
> I hear lake water lapping with low sounds
>   by the shore;
> While I stand on the roadway, or on the pavements
>   grey,
> I hear it in the heart's deep core.

On the planes and in Irish airports, announcements are made in full, flowing sentences with living words: passengers might close their eyes and think they are arriving in a hay-wain. The words draw you in, at least partly because the speaker appears to take pleasure in speaking them.

If the Irish are wise and faithful to their ancestors they will protect this language as fiercely as the French protect theirs, as fiercely as the Italians protect the genes in their tomatoes. Who knows, it might emerge as a competitive economic advantage. Even if it doesn't turn up some improvement in the Irish bottom line, there will still be one airport on earth where they don't say: 'Due to aircraft late arrival, Flight 427 has incurred a twenty-minute delay. Qantas apologises for any inconvenience incurred to you by this delay.' Could they not say to passengers on Flight 427 something like: 'Your plane was twenty minutes late arriving, so it will be a little late to leave. We are sorry for the delay, especially if it has spoiled your plans.' Of course they could not. They have lost the simplest words and the simplest ability to arrange them.

I don't have to be cunning to write misleading sentences, or illiterate to write dead or vapid ones. I only

Rhythm is one of the principal translators between dream and reality. Rhythm might be described as, to the world of sound, what light is to the world of sight. It shapes and gives new meaning. Rhythm was described . . . as melody deprived of pitch.

Edith Sitwell,
Taken Care Of

need be inadequate or unthinking. You cannot write well if you are oblivious to the requirements and possibilities of writing. An untrained painter has more chance of creating something tolerable or interesting than a writer who does not respect the rules of language, or cannot be bothered with the rudiments. The rules are not unbreakable, but they are necessary. There can be no progress – and little joy – without sometimes ignoring or breaking them. Yet they do hold it together. It's much as John Huston said of the rules, or the grammar, of film-making: 'They must, of course, be disavowed and disobeyed from time to time, but one must be aware of their existence . . .'

Take rhythm. Some mastery of sentence structure creates at least the possibility of rhythm in the language. So when did you last hear someone in public life who was not a rapper speak with rhythm? When did you last sense it in a letter from your bank manager? (Well, you probably don't have a bank manager; but if you do, he will not write the way the old ones used to.) Your bank manager – or whatever name his approximation goes by – will have been trained in managerialism, and you can't have both managerialism and rhythm in your sentences. Managerialism exterminates rhythm along with clarity and vigour.

You can be sure your bank-person will not be able to write something that reads half as easily or with as much force as this 400-year-old translation from various 'original sacred tongues': *If a man die, shall he live again? All the days of my appointed time will I wait, till my time come.* Few bank managers ever wrote as well as this; yet there is plenty in it to imitate and, consciously or unconsciously, once upon a time they did. In fact most people who were required to write imitated those cadences. It was possible for a bank manager to be conscious of the beats in language, of the structure of sentences, and of the potential and even the sacredness of language. Such people existed until quite recently, perhaps no more than twenty-five years ago. Coincidentally, their numbers declined not just with the rise of managerialism, but also with the fading of the King James Bible. Even so, if they knew the rudiments, they would see the same sort of rhythm in writers who might be more to their taste, like Elmore Leonard:

> It looked like Tommy had been shot in the head, only one shot hitting him of the five Chili could still hear and count, but the one was enough. Chili stood there not saying a word.

Not everyone can write like this. It's harder than it looks. But everyone who enjoys it can learn from it, and no one who knew anything about language ever said there was one kind of writing for Elmore Leonard and another for an annual report. Someone made that up: and that someone was the progenitor of this:

> An integral aspect of the ongoing management of your investment portfolio is to ensure that the asset allocation of your funds is in line with your risk tolerance, and we would like to take the opportunity to review your risk tolerance and thereby ensure that your portfolio is correctly structured. A person's risk tolerance is the level of risk with which they feel comfortable and enables us to select the right amount of share exposure . . .

Maybe if we were more conscious of the language we wouldn't let them get away with it. Grammar might help. It might even be seen as essential civic instruction: it might put language back in the picture, among the *key strategies* and *core values* and, indeed, *enhanced communications*. And yet, while good grammar should be encouraged, cultivated

One person with a belief is a social power equal to ninety-nine who have only interests.
John Stuart Mill,
Considerations on Representative Government

One ought every day at least, to hear a little song, read a good poem, see a fine picture, and, if it were possible, to speak a few reasonable words.
Goethe, *Apprenticeship*

and hoped for, bad grammar sometimes is more stimulating. Bad grammar can make us laugh, for instance; whereas perfect grammar is frequently the vehicle, if not the foremost weapon, of the pedantic, the humourless and the platitudinous. Much good writing is not as grammarians would have it. Much inspiriting speech is horrifying to their principles. When a young couple stop me in the park so they can stroke my dog, and one of them says swooningly, 'Jeez, his fur is soft as', I know exactly what he means and like it much more than I would have liked some threadbare simile an older person might have added. Soft *as silk, as down, as a baby's bum.*

You hear it all the time now – *cool as, heavy as, stupid as.* Who knows if it comes from their hating similes, or from not being able to think of them? And who cares when it's amusing? We would not want to declare 'as' henceforth something more than a conjunction, but that's the point – grammar has nothing to do with it. Grammar is not where good writing starts: the word is, and the thought provoking it.

An airhead is no less an airhead for having a command of grammar, and a liar is no less a liar. Far from it; the disingenuous, the fatuous and the deceitful are more likely to make headway if they have perfect grammar on their side. Shakespeare has Henry VI say that by erecting a grammar school, 'thou hast most traitorously corrupted the youth of the realm'. Many others have observed that grammar is a means of keeping those without it in their lowly place.

It might strike us as a sign of cultural decline and adds to our reputation for inarticulateness, but we can learn to live with misused words and total confusion about apostrophes: we can suffer *disinterested* for *uninterested*; *fulsome* for *generous* or *full*; *refute* for *reject* or *deny*; and even, with great forbearance, *of* for *have* (*He might of got ten if he had of kicked straight. But there are a lot of 'might ofs' in football, as we know, Tim.*) You can count a dozen little botches of this kind on the radio or in your newspaper every day. Even the errant apostrophes can be tolerated, or solved by simply scrapping them. It is not as if the language was ever fixed, or even logical: spelling, pronunciation, punctuation and meanings have all changed regularly. And we can hardly complain about all the new words when Shakespeare gave us many hundreds of them, including 'pedant'. When we read that a football coach has *strongly annunciated his club's position*, or that *Iraqi boarders are being closely watched*, should we be outraged? Hardly, though you might wonder. Grammar is a concern only when it gets in the way of having, expressing or understanding a thought or perception.

The first draft of this book began: *This is a book about the*

'Megawati has been finally spurned into action.'
ABC Radio

One insider complains: 'In the most recent meeting, we also were told that, as much as possible, we should avoid "caveat-ing" our intelligence assessments' . . . Forget nuance, forget fine distinctions; they only confuse these guys. If that isn't a downright scary dumbing-down of our intelligence product, I don't know what is.
Nicholas D. Kristof, '16 Words, and Counting', New York Times

English language, but not about English grammar. In the current climate it is a wonder I did not write: *This is a book about the English language, but hopefully not about English grammar.* *Hopefully* is the most recent secular representation of God: it has replaced 'God willing' and may be counted as more evidence for the theory that language profits from a deity. Some grammarians will point out that *hopefully* means *with hope* which makes nonsense of my sentence, just as it does when a footballer says, *Hopefully it* (the ankle or groin) *will be okay by Saturday*; or a government minister says, *We're sending troops, but hopefully they will not be needed.* If the minister had said, *but we hope they will not be needed . . . Why* did he not say *we hope?* Why doesn't anyone say *we hope?*

The worst damage, however, is done not by the grammatical flaw but by the word's ubiquitousness. For those living through a plague it hardly matters if the pests are locusts or grasshoppers; what depresses is the number of them. *Hopefully* has become a pestilence. Panting sportsmen, pop stars, vox-popped witnesses to crime and disaster, politicians and talkshow hosts sprinkle it into every second sentence. On some days the ABC cricket commentator, Keith Stackpole, may exceed this ratio, and is even heard to combine it with *in terms of* – as in: *Hopefully in terms of the batting the English might improve somewhat, Tim.*

If people need to learn or recall the principles of grammar, they need only go to Strunk and White's, *The Elements of Style* or Fowler's *Modern English Usage.* It's worth going in any case: you always learn something, no matter how often you open them. Years ago, Strunk

'There has been a lack in terms of numbers of free kicks.'

Football commentator

'In regards to the sensitivity issue . . . '

ABC football commentator

Severe Thunderstorm Advice: Severe thunderstorms which have produced heavy rainfall, large hail and damaging wind have been observed in the Western district this afternoon. These storms are expected to continue. People in the Western district are warned that these storms could produce damaging winds, large hail and heavy rainfall.

Bureau of Meteorology

and White noted how *in terms of* had crept into the language and urged us to forego such 'padding'. Padding is no longer an adequate description. Like the cane toad which kills and substitutes itself for all other species in its path, *in terms of* has wiped out prepositions and participles, corrupted sentences and made much conversation hideous. It is everywhere; from the nation's highest offices to its lowest, throughout the realms of business and the civil service, on the radio, in the street – and in sport, of course. The ABC football expert Stan Alves is Stackpole's winter equivalent and proof that cricket's pedestrian tempo is not to blame. Thus Stanley, 'his words, like cavalry horses answering the bugle, grouping themselves automatically into the familiar dreary pattern', is likely to say things like this: *In terms of the Essendon backline, they're very hard at the ball and all I can say is hopefully the Collingwood players will learn something in terms of their own performance, Tim.* In the wrong hands this sort of language could be used to extract confessions or incite suicide missions. It is too charitable to say that the words are merely superfluous: they are superfluous in the way that cement boots are superfluous to a man in the water. Of course, we can expect ex-footballers and ex-cricketers (and ex-accountants) to murder the language sometimes. They can easily be forgiven, and even thanked for the life and ingenuity they bring to it. Yet we are entitled to wonder why they prefer these tortuous constructions to something like, *I hope the English batting improves, Tim* – which is not only simpler and clearer but, compared to the original, sounds almost moving.

There is always something brave about a verb. When the Civil War general and United States President, Ulysses S. Grant, began to write his *Personal Memoirs* he had massive debts and terminal cancer, but he wrote 250,000 words in the year he had left to him and the work remains a literary marvel and an exemplary military history. Grant had to recount the most complex political and military events. He had to define causes and compute consequences. He did it as he had done when commanding the northern armies, when the lives of men and the fate of the union depended on his meaning being clear. Asked how he did it, he replied – 'with verbs'. As Lincoln used *struggled* at Gettysburg when he might have said *engaged* in battle or *laid down* their lives; or, had he known the modern way, *put their bodies on the line*, Grant wrote with verbs. Of all the things we do need to know about grammar, the verb is first.

Verbs are doing words. Give them up for long enough and chances are you will stop doing anything. Just before he died, the same General Grant wrote a note to his doctor:

Write with nouns and verbs, not with adjectives and adverbs. The adjective hasn't been built that can pull a weak or inaccurate noun out of a tight place.

Strunk and White,
The Elements of Style

'A verb is anything that signifies to be; to do; or to suffer. I signify all three.' If I want to insure against the chance that I will do something despite myself, I should say what I mean, and write *I hope I have not written a book about English grammar*. I should use a verb.

If we ever decide to take grammar seriously again, we may as well bring back elocution, which is its distant relation. Elocution would be worth the trouble if it did nothing more than exterminate the rising inflection. Unknown in this country until the 1970s, great numbers of Australians these days turn all their sentences into questions with this fiendish contrivance. No sentence or sentiment is immune. Simple ones, like, *I was really pumped?* Or, *She had a gun? And she blew his head off with it?* More complex thoughts – *My girlfriend thinks Russell Crowe's a spunk? But I think he's an arsehole?* – may be expressed as two queries in one. Theorising is possible: *It's a small world? And globalisation sort of makes it smaller?* The style suggests doubt, timidity, fear of the categorical, awareness that the mind's grasp of reality is tenuous and the possibility of a fourth dimension must never be discounted: *Just because we can't see it doesn't mean it's not there?*

There is a theory that the tendency developed among baby boomers when they lost God and took to marijuana and sociology. Add to the mix Foucault, Derrida and others beyond the grasp of most young minds but generally rendering belief into something much more relative, and you have a plausible explanation for the problem. *Hopefully*, a reflexive wave to personal humility and unknowable Fate, may have sprung from the same sources. *Hopefully, someone will be able to prove God's real one day?* Until they do, we might wonder if the word and the inflection do not betoken an attempt to impart some energy or meaning to words that profoundly lack these qualities. It doesn't work, of course. As Elmore Leonard said, we should use exclamation marks every 100,000 words or so. He means no device, including gratuitous queries, can raise words from the dead.

Sport is particularly fertile, notwithstanding the invention and vigour it also brings to the language. Nothing breeds clichés like sport, unless it is film and television and celebrity and news and business. Just as we imitate Greg's golf swing, or someone's sidestep or cover drive, we imitate the sportscasters and the sportswriters, and the sportscasters and sportswriters imitate each other. We are like those lost parrots that know they must join another flock or die. We pick up American accents and expressions from watching films and television and in the vicinity of Westminster find ourselves rounding our vowels. Imitating sounds is built-in, irresistible.

From Adelaide to Inverness parents complain that their teenagers are talking like characters in 'Home and Away'. Even our political leaders resort to the comforting banalities of suburban soaps when seeking to comfort the real people who live in the real suburbs. John Howard's *Dear Fellow Australian* letter might have been written by Harold the shopkeeper in 'Neighbours': if ever there was a chap to say *Alert but not alarmed*, it is Harold.

In his autobiography, Czeslaw Milosz writes of a childhood Latin teacher whose classes were 'a Renaissance art of the beautiful arrangement of words'. At his Catholic school in Vilnius students spent as much as an hour translating a single line of verse, until they found the most precise, suggestive, beautiful meaning. In these hours, Milosz says, he learned that 'what one says changes, depending upon how one says it'. There is not much else for my generation to envy in Milosz's pre-war Lithuanian childhood, but I envy him that education in words.

This program is another example of how this organization, comprised of 40 leading companies from 15 business sectors, is continuing to move forward to address its important mission.

Corporate promotion

Discover how you can adopt innovative methods for effectively chartering (sic) future paths for portal development and ultimately make customer interaction . . .

Conference brochure

We might envy it all the more when we watch the evening news, read the newspapers, listen to our political leaders or read a letter from the water company. True, our schools teach that words are capable of different meanings; but they are less inclined to say the difference is made by words and their arrangement than by the context in which they are written, or spoken and, most particularly, heard. It is an axiom of contemporary discourse that context is everything. Whole courses are dedicated to demonstrating the interdependence of text and context – to deconstruction. This is a useful skill. But the skill of connecting words, which is no less useful and surely comes first, is taught nowhere near as widely. Indeed, students of English are more likely to study a film or a television series than anything from the literary canon: everything being a text, everything qualifies. *Hamlet* and 'Who Wants to be a Millionaire' have an equal claim on the modern student's attention: inevitably, in some schools *Hamlet*'s claim is smaller.

English teachers are expected to tell their students how to select *appropriate forms and features, and structures to explore and express ideas and values*. There is nothing in this gush to suggest that in words and their arrangement an idea is sometimes born. Yet people who write know that very often the creative context is the writing itself. You must know what is in your mind when you start, but once started you cannot know in every case what you will come upon. Equally, in the new curriculum there is no suggestion that the words might have an intrinsic value: in the poetry, for example; in explaining an idea, describing a moment. To see how this kind of thinking impoverishes language we need look no further than the

Module B: Critical Study of Texts
This module requires students to explore and evaluate a specific text and its reception in a range of contexts. It develops a student's understanding of questions of textual integrity. (Reread *English Stage 6 Syllabus*, p. 52.)

Students choose *one* text from *one* of the listed types of text.

NSW English Syllabus

SERPENT:
An animal that moves by undulation without legs.
SEMINARY:
The ground where anything is sown to be afterwards transplanted.

Johnson's Dictionary

curriculum itself. It speaks of English as: *experimenting with ways of transforming experience into imaginative texts in different contexts for specified audiences*. Or *Monitoring and assessing the most appropriate technologies and processes for particular purposes of investigating, clarifying, organising and presenting ideas in personal, social, historical, cultural and workplace contexts*. All those things? At the same time?

What happens in schools may happen for different reasons, but it's very like what happens in business and politics. It is no doubt useful to teach children the art of deconstruction. But even if every word of structuralism, post-structuralism and postmodernism were proven true, they are useless if students of ordinary ability do not understand them: and worse than useless if teaching them means not teaching in a way that fosters love for literature and language. Deconstruction is not another word for incomprehensible – or for managerial. But as practised on teenagers now it is just that, and fits neatly with the communications revolution, the managerial revolution, the information revolution, the globalisation revolution: with our age, in other words.

The Australians of my generation were granted a high school and university education that depression, war and an absence of state schools had denied our parents. Our stroke of luck seems more marvellous whenever I see the modern curriculum and course guides: not only did we get an education, and a cheap one, but ours had a broader and more inspiring sweep than the one served to our children. No one had thought to call public investment in education an investment in 'social capital', as if this was the only way to justify it. Our schooling retained more than a ghost of the idea that an education for education's sake was justified, and had nothing to prove in the marketplace. No one had even thought of Media Studies, Cultural Studies, Women's Studies or Communications. We were not expected to *develop knowledge and understanding of the ways in which language forms, features and structures shape meanings in a variety of textual forms* as the current New South Wales English syllabus describes contemporary requirements. Our teachers still believed in language. A text was still an instructional book; a context nothing more than another word for circumstances.

Naturally, not everyone was satisfied by these pure purposes. Shakespeare, history and foreign languages, were all an offence against the utilitarian strain in the culture and all were casually derided by just about everybody, including slow-witted or hormonally deranged youths wanting an excuse to leave. The dogma of vocational education was never far away. We had no chance of getting Latin or Greek: not in the state schools. We spent a few

In the world
of words, the
imagination is one
of the forces of
nature.

Wallace Stevens,
Opus Posthumous

. . . any knowledge
entity is incomplete
if it does not
cultivate a dialog
(sic) between the
members of the
community of
practice to advance
the defining and
refining of a socially
constructed process.

Knowledge Management

hours on Latin roots and a term on *Antigone*, and that pretty well did for the classics. As for grammar, women of unwavering forbearance taught it as a component of the subject called English Expression. My memory, and the unsureness of my grammar, both tell me that it did not impress itself upon us greatly. Perhaps the curriculum should have allowed more time for something so important, but I suspect the problem was less in the system than in us. And less with the teachers: with not a fraction of their dedication we were never going to learn the art of arranging words. That we lacked all motivation had something to do with puberty and sport. But our teachers also had to contend with that general contempt for knowledge that was not 'useful'. Grammar was useful to the extent that it was useful to be understood. There was no harm in knowing how to write a good sentence, especially if you had a bit of a bent for it. But it was not an essential skill, unless you intended to be a teacher yourself. This was rural Australia and necessity governed the mind of it.

Australian pragmatism is not always a good friend of the Australian language. We might occasionally rise to heights of laconic grace and invention, but everyday language was a sort of forcing tool – like a crow-bar or hammer; a practical implement with which one may improvise, elegantly if you were up yourself, but more often brutally. Our teachers stared bravely at our sullen, distracted faces and no doubt pretended to themselves that one day we would be grateful for knowing the difference between a subject and a predicate. They might have gone as far as transitive verbs, but if they did I forgot them long ago. Some of us were curious or dutiful enough to learn the rudiments, but not much more. The 'arrangement of words', like the arrangement of flowers, was at best something to occupy the feminine element, and at worst as useful as tits on a bull. For thinking beyond the rule of necessity, one can never thank one's teachers enough.

If we picked up a feeling for the language it was in English literature: in the English and Australian poets (we studied Hope and Wright but not Eliot and Yeats); in the Austen and Dickens we laboured through; but especially Shakespeare. Shakespeare was the best thing they gave us. *Julius Caesar*, *Macbeth*, *King Lear* and a couple of the sonnets burrowed their way in and took up residence in our inhospitable souls. We never saw the plays performed or even heard them read, but the words came off the page and stuck. It was the one hint we had that there were mysterious powers in language: that beautifully arranged words could liberate, possess, bewilder and intoxicate. They contained revelations. They could extend a person. There was pleasure just in reciting them.

His life was gentle,
  and the elements
So mixed in him
  that
Nature might stand
  up
And say to all the
  world
This was a man.
  William Shakespeare,
    Julius Caesar

My words fly up, my
  thoughts remain
  below:
Words without
  thoughts never to
  heaven go.
  William Shakespeare,
    Hamlet

Standing on the pedals of your pushbike, grinding your way up the hill to home, panting: 'Tomorrow and tomorrow and tomorrow/Creeps in this petty pace from day to day/And all our yesterdays . . .' 'Cowards die many times before their deaths.' 'Let me have men about me that are fat'. 'Out, vile jelly! Where is thy lustre now?'

If I could write the curriculum, I would begin with language: from the first hour of the first day at school, and every day thereafter for twelve years, children would study 'the beautiful arrangement of words'. If at the end of their schooling they could not understand the language of their likely employers, I would feel that some of education's duty had been done. Innocence had prevailed a little longer, and with it hope that the corporate muck might be leached away by a populace in love with the real language. Saved from the advanced objective of modern English to *know and understand the purposes and effects of a range of textual forms in their present social, historical, cultural and workplace contexts*, they might remember poetry, drama and ideas, remain aware of the word's potential and loathe dead language all their lives.

In institutions where we might expect the most resistance the capitulation is most complete. Managerialism came to the universities as the German army came to Poland. Now they talk about *achieved learning outcomes, quality assurance mechanisms* and *international benchmarking*. They throw *triple bottom line, customer satisfaction* and *world class* around with the best of them. The university might have no plausible claim to be among the best in the world. The terms might not describe the normal concerns of knowledge, education and research. The words might not mean any sensible thing. No matter. Those who insist that the words *should* mean something can take the redundancy package and motor off in their Wolseleys. They can sit out their lives reading Plato and drinking cask claret while the real academics get on with teaching *customers* and *strategising* at retreats. It is hilarious. What is truth? Bah! Socrates or Plato? Kant or Nietzsche? Does it really matter? The debates at the centre of Western civilisation are now truly academic because they cannot be conducted in the language of managerialism or taught under managerial criteria in universities. Not only is managerial language inadequate to these fundamental questions about the nature of truth, it has no respect for them. It is not a language for serious inquiry or explanation, or even for thinking.

As Rob Watts, a Melbourne academic has written, the university defines itself in language more imbued with the spirit of public relations than truth-telling. When we read a university's assessment of its graduates we know what he means. According to their *Program Quality Management System* they will: *Act as professionals, meaning they will participate actively and innovatively in their professional and social communities of practice in the context of the developing knowledge economy*. Meanwhile they will also: *Reflect as citizens – reflect upon their actions as engaged citizens in the context of local diversity and multiculturalism, increasing globalisation and the university's commitment to awareness of global sustainability and indigenous issues*. Furthermore, they will: *Learn from experience – make context-sensitive judgements that enable them to continuously develop and transform their practice and themselves*. If ever there was a prefabricated henhouse of prose this is it, and it's one that echoes the

---

Information needs are of various types. Apart from expressed or actualised needs, there are unexpressed needs which a client is aware of, but doesn't like to express. Another category of needs is the dormant variety, which the client is unaware of . . . In order to identify information needs one should adopt various methods to gather information on the various factors that influence the formation of needs. No single method or tool will serve entirely. A careful selection and blending of several techniques depending on the client whose need is being studied is necessary. In fact, the 'information needs identifier' should study, prepare and equip him/her-self thoroughly to perform the task of identifying information needs . . . It is to be noted that methodology will become clearer and clearer as each step is put into practice enhancing the understanding of the scenario and help in fine tuning the procedure to suit particular situations.

From a paper presented to a congress of south-east Asian librarians

totalitarian fantasies Orwell wanted to eradicate. The words are of human origin; but they might also have been written by a not very context-sensitive robot programmed with all the clichés of modern prose and what passes for modern understanding. These are not just graduates: they are the New Citizens of the twenty-first century, or astronauts fitted out for interplanetary travel; or, let's be honest, figments of a failed imagination. It doesn't matter which, because they don't exist. The writer has failed to describe a credible being. It is all humbug. Or, put another way, it is PR. It's marketing: it might not have a lot to do with the genuine prospects of students, but in a competitive world you need ambitions. You've got to want things. And who doesn't want to be capable of continuous transformation *and* aware of indigenous issues?

Marketing, as the marketeers will tell you, is 'rooted in the exchange process'. Increasingly that's where universities are also rooted. And because of this they call their students *clients*, or *customers*, and feel free to sell the virtues of their institutions – real or imagined – like patent medicines. It is part of the business of marketing to muddy the distinction between altruism and cynicism: it is not normally given as part of a university's business to do this, but in taking on the language of marketing it risks taking on this part of its business.

Here are the words of an inquiry into an Australian state economy: . . . *universities face enormous pressures, with no sign of relief on the horizon.* Compare the horizon in this drab sentence, to the one on that same page of Faulkner's *As I Lay Dying* quoted earlier. *The sun, an hour above the horizon, is poised like a bloody egg upon a crest of thunderheads*. We do not want the writers of a report on a state's economy to put bloody eggs on anyone's horizons, but, if only for the exercise, it would do them good to think of a simile of their own. Even if they decide not to use it: at least the effort might lead them to something better than a cliché, two in fact, end on end. No one who is paid to write should write a cliché. Everyone who can write is capable of something better. Just leaving the horizon out of it would help. Or, *no relief can be expected.* And then – it's wonderful what happens once you start – our writer might be led to think twice about *enormous pressures*. Homer, as far as we can tell, managed not to say the Trojans were facing *enormous pressures*. Surrender the tired adjective; the universities are left facing pressures with nothing enormous in the way of them, and at once

---

An insistence on clarity and polish appropriate to a late version is entirely inappropriate to earlier ones meant to get the ideas on paper. Worrying about the rules of writing too early in the process could keep you from saying what you actually had to say . . . I can draw the analogy to the completion of consultancy project assignments . . . The tension between making it better and getting it done appears whenever people have work to finish or a product to get out: a computer, a dinner, a term paper, an automobile, a book.
I like to get it out the door . . . My temperament — impatient, eager for frequent rewards, curious about how others will respond to what I have said — pushes me in that direction. Intellectual life is a dialogue among people interested in the same topic. You can eavesdrop on the conversation and learn from it, but eventually you ought to add something yourself.
From Summary Notes of Howard S. Becker, *Writing for Social Sciences*

you see that, in general, pressures are not something you face. Pressures tend to bear down on you. They're a kind of invisible weight. Pressure crushes. That's why we say we're *under pressure* – *under* is better than *face* even if it leaves us for a moment with something very like a cliché. And if we say *under pressure*, we might be led to say it's like a *vice*, and the *vice* is tightening and no one is going to loosen it. You might say the universities are being squeezed. You might not want to settle on *vice*, but so long as your imagination is engaged and not your storehouse of clichés you are less likely to write the passage that follows:

These pressures include substantially reduced Commonwealth funding, unfavourable democratic trends, and impending Commonwealth initiatives, which, along with reform, may present threats. Added to these pressures is the desire for the universities to be more integrated in the overall economic development strategies of the State.

You get this far and all you know is that any moment now they'll be talking about *challenging environments* and *identifying core issues* and *key issues* (not to say, *key tasks*) and the need for *strategic models*; and that some progress has been made in *deriving synergies between the separate entities*; *but the pace of reform must be accelerated*. In this instance they *are* soon talking about such things, of course – and frankly I don't believe a word of it. It's bunkum. These phrases no more describe what is needed and what is happening in Australian universities than they do what is happening in Kabul: if they did describe it, nothing is needed and nothing is happening because nothing is what they describe. Therefore the writing is useless and the writers should not be paid; but the writers are likely to tell you they were told to write these things by the experts who investigated the *enormous pressures*. Surely this can't be true: they are business people, experts, politicians.

It can only mean that writing and thinking are, if not the same thing, quite inseparable. If you write like porridge you will think like it, and the other way around. And if you have to read porridge all the time you may well begin to speak it, even in extremis: so when your child is killed you may tell the press, as one man did this year, that you can *only pray to God that you will have closure*. Or if your son died in battle and is buried in a mass grave you might say, as the US military imagines, that you are going to be *forever speculative on how he died* when, surely, you're always going to wonder. But then, if you're dealing with the military, you're likely to be told that *living soldiers and non-combatant civilians are higher priorities*; and

About two hundred yards from the German derelicts, which were now furiously belching inky smoke, I looked down into the face of a man lying hunched up in a pit. His expression of agony seemed so acute and urgent, his stare so wild and despairing, that for a moment I thought him alive. He was like a cleverly posed waxwork, for his position suggested a paroxysm, an orgasm of pain. He seemed to move and writhe. But he was stiff. The dust which powdered his face like an actor's lay on his wide open eyes, whose stare held my gaze like the Ancient Mariner's.

Keith Douglas,
'An English Poet in the
Western Desert 1942'

People who are already dead would not be at the top of triage. And if this is your only comfort you might start repeating it to anyone who will listen.

Split infinitives are not the problem with public language. In its modern form there are not enough infinitives to split. They need more verbs. They need to *think* in verbs. The report on universities might have said:

> The universities are under pressure. They have lost funding and they are losing people. They struggle to keep up with the demands of reforming governments and a modern economy. True, changes have been made: they share resources and research and look for other ways to cooperate. But they must do more than this.

Put this way, nothing is lost except pomposity, jargon and platitudes. And several hundred words that no one needed. It's hardly poetry, but it is clearer, and to that extent it lays a claim to prose. After all, as often happens with public language, the sludge will not let us see the drama in what it purports to describe: the drama that sits in all minds, even the minds of those twenty-first century secular Methodists, the technocrats who want us to believe that life is a collection of *key issues* that can be strategically managed into *favourable outcomes*.

The subjects of the report *are* like the Trojans. To begin with, inside the walls of the universities there are people, with psychology and politics about them, and all the unpredictable and startling potential for chaos and enchantment that goes with people. Like the Trojans, they are people *under siege* (which is a more evocative phrase than *pressure*, even *enormous pressure*). Like the

Quality Function Deployment has four phases. Phase one, gathers the voice of the customer, puts its words (sic) accurately understood by producing organization and analyses it versus the capability and strategic plans of the organizations. This means that plans are communicated and conflicts between plans are resolved. Also, each manager monitors his or her plan on a monthly basis and studies successes and problems to make the changes in behavior that will help assure the plan will be met and exceeded.

Management document

Trojans, they have something the besiegers want – not a woman in this case, but their submission certainly. Their hearts and minds? Their heads? Their souls? Something a lot more interesting than *creating deeper centres of excellence at each institution through greater specialisation and achieving implementation success*.

Apart from clarity and shape, what we miss in these words is originality. Because there is no sign the authors have thought about the words, we are not encouraged to think about what they say. As Dr Johnson said, 'What is written without effort is in general read without pleasure.' Nothing in the words suggests that the authors understand the institution they describe, or that they have some feeling for it. There is no personality or character in them. 'Speak that I may see thee': but these words don't speak and we can't see. It is not very long ago that those who ran universities and libraries defined them in their own terms, and defended them by defending learning. Now they parrot words and concepts of corporate management.

The profit from giving the name *clients* or *customers* to people who study in universities and read in libraries is not yet apparent.

It is possible to believe, as this refugee from academia does, that universities were rarely half what they claimed to be and badly needed dragging towards the realities of late-twentieth-century life, yet see no reason why they should give up the language of an institution of learning and take up international management-speak. Do they imagine that the new language is the necessary condition of being *world class*, and that the character of a place has nothing to do with it? That is what this writing lacks – character.

Whatever change necessity demands, universities should continue to respect the idea that truth is something worth pursuing, even when the consensus is they cannot hope to find it. Believing only this much about the truth compels us to respect the language: and it compels universities particularly, because it is a traditional function of universities to respect language and culture, and if they don't respect it now, no one will.

At issue in the decline of public language is a principle like the one defended furiously by supporters of the seventeenth-century King James Bible and the sixteenth-century *Book of Common Prayer*. In the critics' eyes (T.S. Eliot's for instance) the twentieth-century revised versions were exasperatingly pointless and philistine assaults on culture and history the traditional language had preserved. 'Neither cast ye your pearls before swine' became 'Do not feed your pearls to pigs', and there was plenty more where that came from. The translators of the NEB could not have brought more loathing on themselves if they had taken to Ely Cathedral with a Sherman tank: a good deal less in fact, because a cathedral can survive pillaging, and faith can be renewed in the rebuilding, but words once lost are gone forever.

What is more, a cathedral is the property of the church, whereas a language belongs to civilisation, and (as T.S. Eliot might insist) if it is dragged down takes civilisation with it. Language is not just a preserver or bearer of tradition. Words do more than the elemental thing of linking one generation to another. The great works of public language like the *Book of Common Prayer* are poetic works. In the poetry is the mystery which religion concerns and on which it depends. In the poetry the inexpressible is sensed. Many church people will tell you that when it adopted everyday modern prose, the church cut off an artery to its soul.

So their argument goes; and every time we hear a modern marriage celebrated we might agree. 'Those whom God has joined together let no man put asunder', it used to say; and 'With all my worldly goods I thee

Wilt thou have this woman to thy wedded wife, to live together after God's ordinance, in the holy estate of matrimony? Wilt thou love her, comfort her, honour, and keep her in sickness and in health; and, forsaking all other, keep thee unto her, as long as ye both shall live?

Book of Common Prayer,
Solemnisation of
Matrimony

We brought nothing into this world, and it is certain we can carry nothing out . . .

Book of Common Prayer,
The Order for the Burial
of the Dead

endow'. But now they are as likely to say something about partnerships and sharing everything, and it is hard to think of a sensible reason for the change. It's not tradition we miss so much as the ring of truth. Because in the old language is the old truth, the one that the writers found in the words.

Living where he does in times like these, Philip Roth can be forgiven for saying that all public language is a lie. But it is not so – not entirely. The *Book of Common Prayer* from which the old marriage ceremony was drawn – and by more denominations than the Church of England – was public language. Good people have lived by good public language for generations. The power of the *Book of Common Prayer* or the King James Bible lies not in its antiquity, but in the conviction that the words convey. An atheist can still be moved, entertained and enlightened by them. You can enjoy the feel of them in your mouth like a sacrament. As well as any, those works illustrate how public language is *elevated* language: it manifests – and honours – the traditions of the culture. In its highest form it is exemplary language, structurally and morally. It inspires respect, encourages thought and aspiration. It unifies. 'In the midst of life we are in death' are words by which for several centuries millions understood the sad paradox of existence. They are a perfect expression of our predicament, and that's why they are both majestic and comforting. The words have survived, but Thomas Cranmer, who is credited with writing them, was burned at the stake. He was devoured clutching the recantations – the falsehoods, the political correctness – that had been extracted from him.

Possibly, had it come to him in a vision, Cranmer

'And forasmuch as my hand offended, writing contrary to my heart, my hand shall be punished therefore; for, may I come to the fire, it shall be first burned.'
Thomas Cranmer, before
his execution

But still, the fates
will leave me
my voice,
and by my voice I
shall be known.
Ovid, *Metamorphoses*

If there's one word that sums up everything that's gone wrong since the War, it's Workshop.
Kingsley Amis,
Jake's Thing

would have gone willingly to the flames, bearing the revised version as well as the recantations. The rest of us can still ask on his behalf, what did they imagine would be gained by addressing God in the same way we address a parking officer – as *You* instead of *Thou*? As much as we would get by turning Lincoln's classical prose, and classical endeavour to engage both the mind and the emotions, into a PowerPoint presentation; or eliding from Churchill's great speeches all the echoes of Thomas Babington Macaulay. Which is to say nothing would be gained, but our loss would be 'grievous beyond all knowing'.

Every workplace where the written language matters would be happier and more productive if no one wrote sentences like this: *These commitments are consistent with the move to more evidence-based decision making in all natural resource management issues and will address the NCC's outstanding assessment issues regarding water reform.* And there is more to it than clarity and precision and our ability to comprehend and trust our leaders. There is the matter of the culture: of the choice between a dead language and a living one. Not only can the public language be improved, it ought to be improved. Clear, precise, active language is good for democracy and for society. Active language incites activity. It helps to establish trust between the governors and the governed and the managers and the managed. Honesty and good intentions and deceit and incompetence are more easily recognised.

I make my living as a writer, and reading is a necessary and favourite pastime: so I have an interest in these matters. I stress 'interest'. It is not a passion and only on one or two points does it approach obsession; just as writing is for me not obedience to an unstoppable urge or the visceral thing some writers describe. Les Murray's profound personal experience when writing poetry I have not had writing prose. Nothing I've written would lead me to say as Murray does, 'It's done in every part of your muscles – you can feel it in your muscles'. Half his luck, I say. In my muscles I feel only the lack of exercise, and occasionally fear.

And yet I know what he's getting at. There *is* a physical dimension to it. Writing contains mysteries which only exertion can uncover. If you are possessed of rare empathy, or Keats's 'negative capability' and can imagine what it's like to be a sparrow, the task will be easier sometimes. If you are master of your subject, and of writing as well, so much the better. But even for geniuses there will be gruelling times: for those of us less blessed, if it doesn't hurt, probably we're not trying hard enough.

We will not write as well as we can, however, if we make a meal of our deficiencies. We must not be intimidated, but

'It depends on
what the meaning
of "is" is.'
Bill Clinton, *videotaped
evidence to the grand jury*

In prose, the worst
thing one can do
with words is
surrender to them.
George Orwell, *Politics
and the English Language*

I write as well
as I can on each
occasion.
Italo Calvino,
Hermit in Paris

find some agreeable place between awareness of our limitations and submission to them. It helps to know that experience has persuaded many average to good writers that while it is never possible to rise to the level of literary genius if you're not one, you can always improve. In the end everyone who writes can at least share some of a great writer's hopes. We can all, like Czeslaw Milosz, search for 'our home in one sentence'. Milosz discovered in his writing: 'An unnamed need for order, for rhythm, for form, which three words are opposed to chaos and nothingness.' In the same way, everyone who writes, including those employed in marketing, politics and the public service, can recognise writing to which none of these words apply; and writing where chaos and nothingness rule the language that is supposed to be their enemy. Writing, in other words, that has no respect for writing. Everyone who writes can be a critic of writing. Everyone can take some responsibility for the language. Translated to the public language, this is the starting point of my argument, the conceit on which it is built. All writers can improve, so the public language can improve. It is a question of consciousness. And necessity. If it is the right of all citizens to know, it is equally their right to be competently told.

At least with the language tacked together like a prefabricated henhouse, George Orwell was left with something recognisable and accommodating. We have a henhouse that no hen or hen-keeper ever saw before or wanted to see again: an alien, inhospitable, impenetrable henhouse. It is not so much a henhouse as a cage, and we may as well be parrots in it.

Glossary

> . . . and yet his words, like cavalry horses
> answering the bugle, group themselves
> automatically into the familiar dreary pattern.
> This invasion of one's mind by ready-made
> phrases (*lay the foundations, achieve a radical
> transformation*) can only be prevented if one is
> constantly on guard against them, and every such
> phrase anaesthetises a portion of one's brain.
>
> George Orwell,
> *Politics and the English Language*

THE CASE MADE IN this book does not lend itself to barricades and rallies. It does not reduce to slogans; and if it did, who would shout them? People will march to save a cultural institution, some threatened corner of a way of life or a clump of trees, but they will not rally for the language. Not physically at least. I have written this essay in the hope that awareness might increase in some small degree and with it, indignation: a small degree and a not very sanguine hope because I know that powerful forces, including possibly the whole tide of history, are against us. 'Does literature, does reading, does literary analysis, change anything except consciousness?' the critic Don Anderson asked a few years ago: and, answered his own question – sadly, with rare exceptions, *No*.

Substitute 'works of the imagination' for 'poetry', he said, and Auden has it about it right.

> For poetry makes nothing happen: it survives
> In the valley of its making where executives
> Would never want to tamper . . .

The same is true if we substitute my plea for 'imaginative language', or 'language from which the imagination is not excluded', or just 'real language'. Real language makes 'nothing happen': not of itself, not when lousy language will do as well. And executives don't tamper: they live with and on the lousy.

Still, it is not a puny thing to change consciousness; and so long as we are powerless to change experience we'll take it. The greater part of the struggle over language will have to be conducted with language. How else did managerialism impose itself on all our lives if not with words? With marketing, no doubt; and PowerPoint, the profit motive, huge natural advantages and all kinds of tricks including fear. But in words they conveyed the creed which exiles us, and words are the only means of fighting back.

The principal tactic is counter-assertion: they say, *deconfliction*, we say *Claptrap! Hogwash!* And we say it *every* time – mockingly, aggressively, in sorrow, in anger. We can also turn our backs every time they say it, drape our handkerchiefs on our heads or tap our pens furiously. We can try being a refusnik and say we will not answer such a letter, much less send a cheque. And mock them; never stop mocking them.

People seeking a more creative solution might propose in their workplaces a twelve-month moratorium on selected words and phrases. This will improve the public language, first, by ridding it of some dull and stupid pests; second, by obliging writers, speakers and researchers to rediscover good words that have fallen into disuse; and third, by encouraging those responsible for what the rest of us have to read and hear to respect our most precious cultural inheritance. This is a limited preliminary list and the effects will not be immediate. But as more people become conscious of the *issue*, they will stop saying *issue* and search for fresher and more precise words. *Problem* will not do. Reference books will find a way into their lives. They will have conversations about language with their colleagues and friends. Without *issue* to fall back on, they will come up with words like disease, plague, myxomatosis, sclerosis, oedema, predicament and dilemma. Paradox will be rediscovered.

Organisations can set themselves monthly, quarterly and yearly targets for expunging words and discovering them. Inevitably, language consultancies will sprout in every town and city, but they will have to go by a different name, because if ever a word needed abolishing it is *consultant*.

Overall, the effect should one day stand comparison with the desert around Uluru when cattle and other hard-hoofed animals were fenced out: it bloomed into a natural garden of infinite variety. When you see it the wonder is to think this splendour had been there all along, buried, waiting. As language is. Those with no feeling for the natural world might find more inspiration in the example of the free market once liberated from the slovenly and oppressive interventions of governments. The lesson is the same however you learn it: these words clog the language and cut us off from thought, feeling and possibility.

Here are some to set the ball rolling, and some synonyms that also serve as a very modest sample of words that could be substituted for the proscribed ones. A useful exercise is attached to each entry.

In terms of: In relation to, in regard to, in respect of; because, for (As in: I support it *in terms of* the benefits it will bring); insofar, to the extent that; towards, to, about (As in: My attitude *in terms of* the Premier is that he is lying *in terms of* the issue); on (As in: France is likely to exert a lot of influence *in terms of* the final outcome.)

Exercise: Rewrite the following sentence without *in terms of*:

Burke and Wills showed great commitment *in terms of* exploring Australia.

Commitment (commit, committed): An expression of resolve, intent, loyalty, fealty, fidelity, willingness, faith, dedication, devotion, determination etc. An interest or belief in another person, an animal such as a dog or race-horse, a thing, a policy, a club or employer, or oneself, etc. An attachment to someone, something or oneself. A pledge or oath (As in: With this ring I thee *commit* myself to.) Duty. Passion. Obsession. (As in: I have an absolute *commitment* to you, darling.) An intention to do something. (I am *committed* to going to the ends of the earth with you, my precious.)

Exercise: Rewrite the following sentence without *committed*:

At the end of the day Burke and Wills were not *committed* enough.

Enhance (enhancement, enhancing, enhanced): Improve, increase, grow, swell, enlarge, streamline, beautify, strengthen etc.; make more efficient or effective; brighter, weightier, lighter, pointier, hairier, longer, thicker etc. (As in: Our marriage was *enhanced* when Bruce started on the amitryptoline, but then his prostate got *enhanced* and it went backwards.) Make more lifelike, more graphic or more fun (as in sex or violence). The list is as long as human desire, aspiration, talent etc., as deep as the oceans etc., as rich as nature and experience etc.

Exercise: Rewrite the following sentence without *enhancement*:

Dying in the desert was a tragedy for Burke and Wills but an *enhancement* in terms of their status as icons.

Fora (an archaic word, pl. of *forum* revived for no apparent reason in the 1980s, sometimes made pl. as *foras*): Forums (As in: various international *fora*); meetings, conventions, gatherings, conferences; organisations, bodies, groups; parliaments, guilds, associations, clubs etc.

Exercise: Rewrite the following sentence without using *fora*:

Crossing Australia Burke and Wills saw a lot of flora and *fora*.

Key (See *core*): A thing with which to open something, especially a door or window; the reason for success; to type something in (vb); core (adj) (As in: *key* promise, *key* initiative, *key* decision, *key* strategy, *key* commitment etc.); the central, most efficacious, most demanding thing; crucial, decisive, essential, fundamental, most important, the best, cleverest, the one we want to stress, spend the most money on etc.

Exercise: Rewrite the following sentence without using *key* (or *core*):

Burke now took a *key* initiative, and committed himself to no more than three quarters of a bottle a day.

Core (See *key*): The centre, heart or truth of something, the bit you throw away, not. (*Core* policy, *core* commitment, *core* strategy etc.) The hard, pithy or stringy bit. The essential thing about it. Also ***non-core*** (As in: That was a *non-core* promise.)

Exercise: Rewrite the following sentence without *core* (or *key*):

The commitment I made not to introduce a GST was not a core promise, but a non-core promise.

Strategic: (adj) strategy (n) strategise, strategising (vb) strategically (adv). Clever, smart, far-sighted, very clever (as in a *strategic* plan, policy campaign etc.) Anything better than stupid, misguided, wrong etc. Well-planned, well-husbanded, well-marshalled. Tactical, considered, measured etc. Antonyms: non-strategic, unstrategic, myopic, playing it by ear, ad hoc, flexible, adaptable, free, light on one's feet, exceedingly clever.

Exercise: Rewrite the following sentence without using *strategy*:

Burke and Wills tried hard but at the end of the day what they lacked was a key *strategy*.

Hopefully: With hope. Full of hope. With luck. With a bit of luck. I/we/they etc. hope. If we're lucky. God willing. With every confident expectation. Here's hoping. With hope in our hearts. Here's looking up your kilt. Barring accident. Hope, hoping, hopeful (As in: I hope you are well. Hoping to hear from you soon. I am hopeful.) Also – wish, desire, expect, anticipate etc.

Exercise: Rewrite the following sentence with *hopefully* nowhere to be seen:

Hopefully, Wills' faith was justified and at the end of the day there is life after death.

Prioritise: To give precedence to. To put or do first. To attend to a task in preference to another. Rate above others. Above all. Rank according to importance, urgency, affection etc. (As in: I'm sorry Thelma, but I've *prioritised* Jennifer in terms of my desire.) To judge foremost, paramount, pre-eminent, principal, main, essential, vital, the thing that matters now. Prior (As in: I can't join you tonight because I have a *prioritised* commitment.) Foremost.

Exercise: Rewrite the following sentence without using *prioritise*:

Burke and Wills *prioritised* their needs with those of their camels.

Outcome: Result, consequence, end, upshot, effect, conclusion, product etc. What comes out of strategising; hence, triumph, victory, good show, bottler etc. Disaster, calamity, fizzer, net-negative, down the gurgler, not worth a crumpet, excellent not, I don't think so, etc.

Exercise: Rewrite the following sentence with *outcome* (and other offending words) out of it:

Hopefully, Burke and Wills were not too disappointed in terms of the final *outcome*.

Issue: That (anything) which you or your company has with another individual or company. The important matter or question to be resolved. Where the weight is. Also any problem, argument, complaint, difficulty, wound, sore spot, bone of contention, bone to pick, difference of opinion or belief etc. (As in: I don't have an *issue* with you or Golden Crumpets Pty Ltd, Jeremy, but I think you might have an *issue* with me.) Whatever is going on between people – inc. rivalry, envy, lust (inc. financial lust), non-payment of debts, lack of empowerment, lack of commitment etc. Issues are core and non-core, key and non-key.

Exercise: What *was* the issue with Hamlet?

To be or not to be; that is the issue.

Empower: To give power. Empowered. Empowerment, inc. self-empowerment (n), empowering (adj), strengthen, vivify, revive, enliven, liberate, make confident, effectual etc. (As in: Brave Achilles *empowered* Patroclus by giving him his shield. Jesus *empowered* Lazarus by raising him from the dead. Harry *empowered* Glenda by giving her the cheque book. A kiss *empowered* Sleeping Beauty who had been *disempowered* by a witch.) Employment, authority, tolerance, psychoanalysis, religion, a PhD, pethidine and nuclear weapons are all said to *empower* people. To validate, approve, justify, a wink and a nod, condone, suck, dog whistle etc. (As in: bigotry, prejudice, greed, malpractice, theft etc.)

Exercise: Rewrite the following sentence as if you had never heard of *empowerment*:

Hamlet had an issue in terms of *empowering* himself.

Impact (verb; also noun, becoming rarer): To run, crash, thump, bang etc. into. (As in: We don't know how the drought will *impact* on farmers' bottom lines.) Affect, change, alter, shift, reshape etc. the economy, the land-scape, the airline industry, the Country Women's Association, football, the national identity, one's per-sonal identity, one's hair, etc. Remake, transmogrify, transform, surprise, spruce up, let down etc.

Exercise: Open your favourite Stephen King novel and substitute *impact* for the first seventeen verbs. Read aloud.

Product: Something that is produced, manufactured, grown, devised, invented, concocted, bequeathed etc. Goods, chattels, potatoes, ideas, concepts, socks, secret intelligence, tourist promotions, education, books, plays and paintings, weather forecasts, greyhound races. Anything. (As in: In fact, New South Wales is coming up with a lot of new *product* in terms of tourism.)

Exercise: Correct this sentence:

There is more product in heaven and earth, Horatio/Than is dreamt of in your philosophy.

Going forwards: In future, the future, trajectory, not regressing or stalled, going on (ongoing), what generally happens without anyone needing to say so. (As in: We have a strategy for continuous improvement outcomes *going forwards*.)

Exercise: Insert *going forwards* in this sentence:

And God said, Let there be light: and there was light.

Input (noun and verb): Contribution, offering, assistance, help, advice, say, suggestion, something put in. (As in: I would like to thank Gerard for his robust *input* tonight; or (vb) If I may *input* a suggestion at this point in time.)

Exercise: What is wrong with this sentence?

Great and manifold were the *inputs*, most dread Sovereign, which Almighty God, the Father of all mercies, bestowed upon the people of England . . .

Point in time: Now, then, before, later, presently, earlier, in August, at 12.15. (As in: I didn't know at that *point in time* and I don't know at this *point in time*.)

Exercise: Correct these sentences:

(i) Excuse me, can you tell me the *point in time*?

(ii) At that *point in time* was the word.

Scenario: Summary, outline or précis of a dramatic work or hypothetical or future events. Summary, outline or précis of past and present events. Any events real, projected or fancied. Any circumstances ditto. (As in: It is not possible to give you a pay rise in the present *scenario*, Kylie, but in some future *scenario* it might be going forwards.)

Exercise: What's wrong with the following sentence:

To be, or not to be? They are the *scenarios*.

Implement: Do, realise, make happen, institute, put in train, create, give expression or effect to. (As in: This offer is all part of our strategy of continuous improvement we are committed to *implementing*.)

Exercise: Implement this in the original:

And God said unto Noah . . . *implement* thee an ark of gopher wood . . . And Noah *implemented* three sons, Shem, Ham and Japheth.

Market/marketing: Inform, encourage, persuade, sell, soft-soap, flog, media management/relations, manipulate, harass, spin, exaggerate, distort, bribe, blackmail, lure, frighten, deceive, lie etc. (As in: There is nothing so vile that it can't be *marketed*.)

Exercise: Think of something better to say than this:

Whatever other issues you might have with Goebbels, he had a genuis for *marketing*.

Acknowledgements

MOST OF THE MATERIAL for this book has been drawn from my own experience; as a speechwriter, as a customer, a rate-payer, a voter, a reader of newspapers, an observer of sports, a frequenter of streets, a victim of television and the internet, a citizen. What I did not glean myself, other people sent me, mainly from the places where they work. In this way they added to the quality and variety of my exhibits, and at the same time assured me that I was not a crank. In the last few years I have met hundreds of people who share my concern. They have been teachers and students, public and private employees, people with telephones, bank accounts and insurance policies, customers, consumers – all kinds of people. I thank all of them for helping me; or being, as they say everywhere these days, so *supportive*.

My wife Hilary McPhee was not only *supportive*; the book was her idea. For that and much else I thank her once again. Jane Palfreyman was very *supportive* too; in fact, as a publisher she is the *benchmark in terms of*

193

supportiveness. Rose Creswell was also *supportive* and I thank her as well, along with Murray Bail for his usual stimulation; Karen Pryor for a couple of gems, Helen Smith and Nadine Davidoff.

Also Bruce Petty for doing me the honour of the end-papers.

And Sandy Hollway who, years ago, when everyone else seemed content with the existing *scenario*, agreed with me that there was something rotten in the public language, and faxed an example from the Department of Finance which has been an inspiration and a keepsake ever since.

Given the within year and budget time flexibility accorded to the science agencies in the determination of resource allocation from within their global budget, a multi-parameter approach to maintaining the agencies budgets in real terms is not appropriate.

This is a true, possibly *world class*, death sentence, and I am pleased to give it a home at last.

Bibliography

Peter F. Alexander, *Les Murray: A Life in Progress*, Oxford University Press, 2000.

Jean Amery, *At the Mind's Limits: Contemplations by a Survivor of Auschwitz and its Realities*, Indiana University Press, 1977.

Martin Amis, *The War Against Cliché*, Vintage, 2002.

Don Anderson, 'Angel of Devastation' in *Text and Sex*, Vintage, 1995.

Anonymous, *Primary Colors: A Novel of Politics*, Random House, 1996.

Hannah Arendt, *On Revolution*, Viking, 1965.

Alan Atkinson, *The Commonwealth of Speech. An Argument About Australia's Past, Present and Future*, Australian Scholarly Publishing, 2002.

W. H. Auden, *Collected Shorted Poems 1930–1934*, Faber, 1944.

Francis Bacon, *Essays*, J. M. Dent, 1999.

Richard Brockheiser, *Atlantic Monthly*, in *Australian Financial Review*, 28 March 2003.

Bill Bryson, *Mother Tongue*, Penguin, 1991.

Robert Burchfield, *The English Language*, Oxford University Press, 1985.

Italo Calvino, *Hermit in Paris*, Jonathan Cape, 2003.

John Carey (ed.), *The Faber Book of Reportage*, Faber, 1987.

Jean-Claude Carrière, *The Secret Language of Film*, Faber, 1995.

Manning Clark, *Select Documents in Australian History*, Melbourne University Press, 1980.

Walter de la Mare, *Stories from the Bible*, Faber (n.d).

Joan Didion, *Political Fictions*, Knopf, 2001.

Joan Didion, 'Fixed Opinions, or The Hinge of History', *New York Review of Books*, 16 January 2003.

T. S. Eliot, 'The Hippopotamus', *Collected Poems 1909–1935*, Faber, 1951.

William Faulkner, *As I Lay Dying*, Vintage, 1996.

Gustave Flaubert, *Dictionary of Received Ideas*, Penguin, 1976.

Eduardo de la Fuente, 'Where is Politics at the End of History?', *Arena*, Feb/March 1996.

Ulysses S. Grant, *Personal Memoirs*, Penguin, 1999.

Ernest Hemingway, *A Farewell to Arms*, Jonathan Cape, 1999.

Dorothy Herrmann, *S. J. Perelman: A Life*, Macmillan, 1988.

Homer, *The Odyssey* (translated by Robert Fagles), Penguin, 1997.

Michael Ignatieff, *The Needs of Strangers*, Chatto and Windus, 1984.

Elmore Leonard, *Be Cool*, Penguin, 1999.

Primo Levi, *Other People's Trades*, Simon & Schuster, 1989.

Norman Mailer, *The Armies of the Night*, Signet, 1968.

David Marr and Marion Wilkinson, *Dark Victory*, Allen and Unwin, 2003.

Louis Menand, 'Comp. Time', *New Yorker*, 11 September 2001.

Czeslaw Milosz, *Native Realm: A Search for Self-Definition*, Farrar, Strauss, Giroux, 2002.

Robert T. Oliver, *The Influence of Rhetoric in the Shaping of Great Britain*, Associated University Presses, 1986.

George Orwell, 'Politics and the English Language', in *Inside the Whale and Other Essays*, Penguin, 1962.

George Orwell, *Animal Farm*, Longmans, 1962.

Dennis Potter, *Potter on Potter* (ed. Graham Fuller), Faber, 1993.

Christopher Ricks and Leonard Michaels (eds.), *The State of the Language*, University of California Press, 1990.

Philip Roth, quoted in *Telegraph*, 5 October 2002.

William Safire, *Lend Me Your Ears: Great Speeches in History*, Norton, 1997.

Earl Shorris, *Harpers*, August 2000.

Russell Smith, 'The New Newspeak', *New York Review of Books*, 29 May 2003.

Lytton Strachey, *Elisabeth and Essex*, Penguin, 1971.

William Strunk Jr. and E.B. White, *The Elements of Style* (Third Edition), Macmillan, 1979.

A.J.P. Taylor, *Essays in English History*, Penguin, 1991.

Rob Watts, 'Down and Out . . .', *Journal of Institutional Research*, Oct-Nov 2003.

Simone Weil, 'The Iliad, Poem of Might', 1940–41.

Patrick White, *The Aunt's Story*, Vintage, 1994.

Oscar Wilde, *De Profundis and other writings*, Penguin, 1973.

Garry Wills, *Lincoln at Gettysburg*, Simon & Schuster, 1992.

Keith Windshuttle and Elizabeth Elliott, *Writing, Researching and Communicating*, Irwin/McGraw Hill, 2002.

W. B. Yeats 'The Lake Isle of Innisfree', 'An Irish Airman Foresees His Death', *Collected Poems*, Macmillan, 1955.